GOSPEL
NOTES
and More

For the Twenty-first Century

Harry Houldsworth

Grosvenor House
Publishing Limited

This book is published by
Grosvenor House Publishing Ltd
Link House
140 The Broadway, Tolworth, Surrey, KT6 7HT.
www.grosvenorhousepublishing.co.uk

A CIP record for this book
is available from the British Library

ISBN 978-1-80381-145-1

NOTES also cover: the *Acts of the Apostles*, Letters to the *Romans, Corinthians, Galatians, Ephesians, Philippians, Colossians, Thessalonians, Timothy, Titus, Philemon, Hebrews*, and the Letters of *James, Peter, John* and *Jude*.

CONTENTS

PREFACE

This book was written as a Covid activity.

I am a long-retired lecturer in higher education, and a member of the Progressive Christianity Network Britain. (See the PCN website for blogs written by Harry Houldsworth.) (www.pcnbritain.org.uk)

I differ from many other 'progressive' Christians in believing that modern approaches to Christianity do not necessarily involve a rejection of orthodox views and practices. My view is that we all are unique in the way we come to faith and that people with very different interpretations of the Bible need to love one another and identify shared values.

Gospel Notes and More is a companion book to another Covid activity of mine – the private publication of *Jesus' Story – for a Thoughtful Generation* (email me at houldken@gmail.com for further details) – and aims to provide a comprehensive guide to the biblical sources that support my approach.

There is zero 'preaching' in this book, and it is my hope that *Gospel Notes and More* will quickly speak for itself and be enjoyed by experts and amateurs alike.

Harry Houldsworth, Wetwang. May 2022

*

INTRODUCTION

On Christmas Day, millions of Christians meet in churches to celebrate the birth of Jesus in Bethlehem, and on Easter Sunday they proclaim the Resurrection of Jesus Christ.

It is acknowledged that many Christians still understand Jesus' birth and resurrection in strict biblical ways. This is their right.

However, all Christians in the twenty-first century need to be aware that others see biblical stories in different ways. These *others* may describe themselves as non-orthodox Christians, as Jews, Muslims, Hindus, Buddhists, believers in Nature-based religions, as agnostics or atheists.

It was acknowledged in the Gospels, that even the disciples were initially unable to accept the idea that Jesus was alive again after Easter Sunday, and the Jewish authorities were quick to suggest that the Christians had stolen the body of Jesus from the tomb. So, alternative ways of thinking about the contents of the Bible, have been around for a very long time.

Critically, an increasing number of younger people in the western world are being educated to look upon ancient religions and superstitions with some skepticism, and to reject non-scientific reasoning and supernatural explanations. It follows that there is a growing need for further objective examinations of the life of Jesus within the context of the period in which he lived.

This alternative focus can encourage a larger number of ordinary people to take an interest in Jesus, as someone who has had a major influence on the evolution of thought in the western world.

Jesus was a teacher, a healer, a philosopher and a prophet, whose message about life is largely universal in character.

Jesus' philosophy is still relevant today. His ideas can help many of us, as we attempt in our own individual way to come to terms with existence, struggle to achieve peace of mind, or explore ways to build better communities at home, or even attempt to promote peace on earth. Can we do this before humans destroy life on earth?

The unnecessary war in the Ukraine is only the latest catastrophe to demonstrate that none of us exists in a protected bubble. This year, the war is in east Ukraine; next year it may be on our doorstep, in the East Midlands.

All of us need to look for solutions to these problems: solutions developed around the values of unselfish love to be found at the heart of the many of the great religions and cultures in the world.

I started to promote this wider debate as a Covid Lockdown activity. The result was a book: *Jesus' Story – For a Thoughtful Generation*, which was privately published in May 2021.

Jesus' Story is short (215 pages), easy-to-read, conversational in style, not too academic, and broad in scope. It covers 3000 years of the progressive development of ideas associated with Jesus of Nazareth. However, because of its conversational style, the book cannot fully identify the detailed biblical basis of much of the book's message. This is what *Gospel Notes* does, with few, if any, frills.

The *Notes* cover the content of the three Synoptic Gospels of Matthew, Mark, and Luke. Also included are further notes on the Gospel of John, *Acts of the Apostles,* and on the many apostles' *Letters* included in the *New Testament*. The *Notes* identify issues and questions that, sadly, are rarely referred to in sermons in churches, or in the *New Bible Commentary* – that well-respected reference text frequently used by members of the clergy.

Religious debate did not end with the *Acts of the Apostles,* although one could be forgiven for thinking that – given the popular *Lectionary Readings* used in churches, which make little reference to other religions, or to the last two hundred years of scientific inquiry.

Gospel Notes is designed as a contribution to filling this void. It identifies many discussion topics that need a greater airing (if there is to be any hope of attracting more people into churches in the western world).

While *Jesus' Story – For a Thoughtful Generation*, and *Gospel Notes*, have been produced to encourage further discussions about Christianity and its relevance today, they have also been written to obtain feedback from readers.

Please note that these *Notes* give my own personal testimony (which is all any church member can ever do successfully). I am saying, 'This is how I see it; how do you see it?'

Please write to me at houldken@gmail.com. If possible, I shall reply.

Finally, the *Gospel Notes* are what they say they are – just 'Notes'. They are set down in a random way – and are not always consistent in style. Please focus on the content rather than the style of the *Notes* and decide if they are speaking for you.

As indicated above, these *Notes* offer a personal testimony. There is no suggestion that others should agree with me, except where they recognize that my perceptions are in harmony with their own.

As indicated above, the underlying premise is that we all come to our understanding of the Bible in our own unique way and that the principal requirement for everyone is to demonstrate that honesty of interpretation which was advocated many years ago by John A T Robinson, a former Bishop of Woolwich.

PART ONE

NOTES ON THE SYNOPTIC GOSPELS: MATTHEW, MARK, AND LUKE

These 'Notes' acknowledge and largely utilize the sequence of themes employed in editions of *Gospel Parallels*, published in Nashville, Tennessee, by Thomas Nelson, Inc.

All the editions of *Gospel Parallels* (since the first edition in 1946) provide an easy way to compare the content of the three Synoptic Gospels, story by story.

Gospel Parallels is recommended as reference reading to these 'Notes'. Alternatively, readers may refer to the three individual Gospels of Matthew, Mark, and Luke in any of the popular editions of the *Holy Bible*.

NOTES BY HARRY HOULDSWORTH

1.001: The Prologue to Luke's Gospel (Luke 1:1-4)

Luke's Gospel was written to Theophilus – a Greek-speaking gentile – setting out the 'facts' as known to the author. Written, probably, in the later part of the first century AD, the context is the spread of Christianity away from Palestine in many cities in the Roman Empire

1.002: The Genealogy of Jesus in Matthew (Matthew 1:1-17)

The first theme in Matthew's Gospel is the genealogy of Jesus to confirm that Jesus' family is of the House of David, from which the expected Messiah would come.

Matthew starts with Abraham and has fourteen generations from Abraham to David, fourteen generations from David to the deportation to Babylon, and fourteen generations from Babylon to Jesus as the Messiah.

Thus, the family line is enhanced by a pattern of three groups of fourteen, which is the sort of pattern that would have impressed readers in the Roman period. What was missing, of course, is evidence of the direct bloodline. In the Bible, Jesus was born of Mary by the Holy Spirit and was adopted by Joseph. Later reference in Nazareth to Jesus being the 'son of Mary', rather than 'son of Joseph' suggests that Jesus' parentage was a source of debate during his lifetime.

[*Note that in 1 Timothy, Chapter 1, Paul warns about false teachers offering 'myths and endless genealogies' that promote 'controversies', rather than God's work which is by faith. Does this warning link to the genealogy in Matthew?*]

1.003: John the Baptist's Birth (Luke 1:5-25)

John the Baptist's birth is heralded by the angel Gabriel, to Elizabeth who was elderly and described as 'barren'.

[*This is the sort of detail that would have impressed readers 2000 years ago. It was the type of action they expected of God. Today, supernatural explanations make many people skeptical.*]

1.004: The Birth of Jesus (Luke 1:26-38)

The angel Gabriel visits Mary, the mother of Jesus.

Millions still believe in the Virgin Birth and the Christian Church stresses the Virgin Birth as a fact, but as indicated above, an increasing number of people in the twenty-first century are skeptical about any supernatural explanations.

[*Should this skepticism be acknowledged, directly by the Church, to make churchgoing and a study of the Bible more tempting to people in modern westernized societies that are now intensively multicultural in character and scientific in approach to education?*]

Christians who understand the Holy Bible as 'God-breathed' often have had their faith strengthened by a religious experience of a deeply personal nature. They should see themselves as particularly blessed and understand that without their direct 'experience', they also might view some biblical stories in a non-orthodox light.

1.005: Mary's visit to Elizabeth (Luke 1:39-56)

Mary, the future mother of Jesus, stays for about three months with the pregnant Elizabeth, who became the mother of John the Baptist. Both women are reported to have been full of joy and they praised God for their good fortune. Mary says the words of the 'Magnificat.'

[*This family connection between Jesus and John the Baptist suggests that the 'family' was identified by people of influence in Palestine, who were attempting to find the expected 'Messiah', much as the monks in Tibet searched for the last Dalai Lama.*]

[*This is the first hint in the New Testament that John the Baptist and Jesus may have had powerful promoters, whose activities remain hidden and unexplained in the Biblical story.*]

1.006: The Birth of the Baptist (Luke 1:57-80)

Luke continues his story with a detailed explanation of the birth and naming of John.

Zechariah prophesies that God will raise up a mighty Saviour in the house of David, as spoken of by the prophets, who will save Israel from its enemies. John will go before the 'Lord' (Jesus) and prepare his way and give knowledge of salvation to his people by the forgiveness of their sins.

[*It is interesting that the context here is the renewal of Israel, not the start of a world-wide religion.*]

[*It is also significant that the 'Saviour' did not save Israel from its enemies.*]

1.007: The Birth of Jesus (Matthew 1:18-25 and 2:1-23)

This beautiful story has been treasured by Christians for 2000 years, yet some modern scholars suggest that Jesus was probably born in Nazareth and that the whole purpose of Matthew's birth narrative was to link Jesus' life and death to prophecies in ancient Scripture.

If this is the case, the importance of this story rests on the fact that it has been sincerely believed by generations of Christians. It has played a major role in identifying key 'truths' about Christianity.

Mary Joseph and Jesus are identified as an ordinary family. Jesus is born in poor circumstances in a stable, not as a prince in a palace, and this was a truly new concept. Everybody, then, could identify with the stable, the straw, and the animals.

[*All that is suggested here is that the Church needs to accept in a relaxed way that westernized people in the twenty-first century are now often skeptical about accepting supernatural explanations.*]

Young people today are often inclined to follow the approach adopted by modern historians such as Michael Grant (*Jesus,* Rigal Publications, 1977) or even earlier by President Thomas Jefferson in the *Jefferson Bible* and treat all biblical elements that involve the supernatural as indicating the gulf between how things were interpreted in the past and how they are interpreted today in scientific investigations or by modern historians.]

1.008: The Birth of Jesus in Luke (Luke 2:1-20)

Luke's magnificent story tells us Joseph had to go to Bethlehem for the census, while Quirinius was governor of Syria. Jesus was born in a manger and, outside, shepherds saw a host of angels in the sky. The angels told them of the birth of the expected Messiah in the manger.

[*Was this how Luke imagined the birth of the Messiah might have occurred? He may have believed that God would have done something very special to give a sign of the real 'Messiah's' birth? Why not have angels in the sky? Many people then believed in angels with wings.*]

1.009: The Circumcision of Jesus and in the Temple (Luke 2:21-40)

Luke says that Jesus was brought to Jerusalem, having been circumcised when he was eight days old and having been named 'Jesus' in accordance with angelic instructions.

At the Temple, an old man, Simeon, identified Jesus as the future Messiah and he praised the Lord. Also, an elderly woman, called Anna, who spent her time in the Temple worshipping God, also spoke about Jesus and who he was.

[*Thus, Jesus was identified as the expected Messiah of Israel – but not necessarily as the founder of an international church.*]

1.010: Jesus at the age of Twelve (Luke 2:41-52)

Luke completes his early history of Jesus with the story of Jesus being brought again to the Temple in Jerusalem, at the age of twelve, for the Passover festival. Joseph and Mary accidentally leave Jesus behind and have to return to the Temple, where they find Jesus asking questions of the teachers. Jesus said that he was in his 'Father's house', but Luke suggests that Joseph and Mary did not understand this (which is strange, given the Bethlehem birth story).

This Temple story supports that the claim that Jesus was interested in Scripture from a very early age.

[*There is no direct evidence that he was being groomed by unnamed, important promoters for his future role, but this is a possibility, even if the details are not provided. Jesus was possibly being encouraged, even being trained, as a future teacher or Messiah, by senior persons in the Hebrew hierarchy.*]

THE GALILEAN SECTION

1.011: John the Baptist Preaching (Matthew 3:1-8) (Mark 1:1-6) (Luke 3:1-6)

This is the early history of John preaching in the wilderness and proclaiming a baptism of repentance for the forgiveness of sins.

Later, John identified the Pharisees and Sadducees, collectively, as a 'brood of vipers'. (Matthew 3:7-10) (Luke 3: 7-8)

This indicates that the Gospel writers had decided that the Pharisees and the Sadducees should be cast as the 'enemies' of Jesus.

1.012: John's Preaching to Special Groups (Luke 3:10-14)

'And the crowds asked him, "What should we do?"' In reply John the Baptist said to them, "Whoever has two coats must share with anyone who has none; and whoever has food must do likewise." Even tax collectors came to be baptized, and they asked him, "Teacher, what should we do?" "Collect no more than the amount prescribed for you." Soldiers also asked him, "And what should we do?" He said to them, "Do not extort money from anyone by threats and false accusation and be satisfied with your wages."'

[*John was telling people always to be fair in the way they dealt with others and go out of their way to help those in need. It was simple, practical advice about how to lead a righteous life.*]

[John saw this as following the wishes of God, but what I find striking is that his advice has universal application, irrespective of someone's nationality or creed.]

John the Baptist believed that if you deal with others fairly and help those in need, you will promote the sort of harmony in society that God wishes us to promote, thus giving others a reason to adopt a similar approach. His theme was that loving rather than hating people will eventually transform a community for the better.

<u>It is noteworthy what John did **not** say:</u>

He did not tell people to go into the synagogue and start praying, or to go into the Temple in Jerusalem and pay to kill birds and beasts to be sacrificed to God. He told them, very simply, to repent and change their way of life.

He did not tell them to follow specific Jewish laws or practices, but he encouraged his fellow Jews to think about situations and use their common sense, about ways to promote harmony in society. He could have been advising citizens of any religion in any country in the world.

[John the Baptist's advice was universal in character, like much of Jesus' later teaching. This needs to be acknowledged: his teaching might have been offered to Jews, but its relevance was worldwide. This is the essence of later Christianity.]

John believed in the urgent need for everyone to recognize the simple errors in the way they were leading their lives, to repent and advertise to others that they were starting a new chapter in the lives by being baptized (by being cleansed) in the river Jordan.

John was using a simple but dramatic metaphor. In the same way that water can be used to wash the body at the end of a working day, in baptism, water highlights one's need also to repent and clean the mind (the spirit), in preparation for the imminent 'kingdom of God' – where people will live together in harmony, obedient to God as their king.

John was later imprisoned by Herod Antipas because he had criticized the king on various occasions.

[It is worth noting that John, like many of his Jewish contemporaries, would have had a three-tiered vision of the universe – in which God lived above Sun, the Moon, the clouds and stars, in a realm called 'heaven'. The earth was believed to be flat, and often imagined as having four corners, and beneath the earth was a fiery region known as Hades or Hell, which was the place where some believed, the wicked were sent after death.

God was imagined by the Hebrews as a great king or emperor who (like an earthly king) demanded obedience, especially from the Ancient Hebrews, who were his 'chosen people'.

Satan was a former angel, now opposed to God, whose mission was to turn human beings away from God.

It is important to understand that John the Baptist (like Jesus) placed great emphasis upon one's willingness to believe that living a life of unselfish love and service to others is the prerequisite for membership in the kingdom of God. Neither John nor Jesus mentioned the importance of temple worship, or of ritual or of liturgy.]

1.013: The Baptism of Jesus (Matthew 3:13-17) (Mark 1:9-11) (Luke 3:21-22)

Matthew says that Jesus came from Galilee to John the Baptist, to be baptized by John. (*One assumes that both knew exactly what was to about to happen?*)

John baptized Jesus, and as he came out of the water, the heavens opened and the Spirit of God descended 'like a dove' and alighted on Jesus, and a voice from heaven was heard saying, 'This is my Son, the Beloved, with whom I am well pleased.'

[Millions of Christians still understand this as a historical event, but if this happened then, why can similar supernatural occurrences not be observed from time to time, today, by ordinary crowds? Or was it always intended as something

imaginary or poetic in character: simply a literary technique devised by the authors to advertise the special status of Jesus? Each of us must decide.]

1.014: Jesus' Temptation (Matthew 4:1-11) (Mark 1: 12-15) (Luke 4:1-13)

There are no witnesses here, so one must assume that the temptations of Jesus by the devil are as imagined by the Gospel authors.

The story is too fantastical in character to be believed by many modern persons. The story includes supernatural aspects that were expected and readily accepted by people in the Roman world of Jesus.

What is significant is that Mark suggests that Jesus was driven out by the Spirit into the wilderness for forty days, where he was tempted by Satan.

Forty days would be more than sufficient to allow any person think clearly about their mission in life. Forty is a repeated number in the Bible and reminds readers of other biblical stories. The number is a literary device.

[*The idea of withdrawing into a quiet area, to reflect and pray, was much practiced by John the Baptist and Jesus, and it tells us a great deal about how they understood that prayer was more about listening and imagining what God was saying to them, than about standing in crowds, shouting out words and making a great noise.*]

1.015: Jesus in Galilee (Matthew 4:12-17) (Mark 1:14-15) (Luke 4:14-15)

The arrest of John the Baptist provided a clear warning to Jesus of the dangers of offending those in authority. He moved away from Herod Antipas' territory into Galilee. There, he preached in the synagogues about the coming of the kingdom of Heaven and the need for repentance. (Luke 4:14,15) He was repeating what John the Baptist had been teaching.

1.016: Rejection at Nazareth (Matthew 13:54-58) (Mark:6-6a) (Luke 4:16-30)

Jesus preached in his hometown of Nazareth and said that he had been sent to bring good news to the poor, to proclaim the release of captives, to let the oppressed go free, and declare the 'year of the Lord's favour.' (Luke 4:16-19)

[*The background here is biblical. People held captive in Jesus' life were often people like John the Baptist, in prison because he had offended a local ruler. Many people were also 'oppressed'. Jesus wanted to free the oppressed. The 'year of the Lord's favour' implies that something important to the Jews would happen that year, whenever it occurred.*]

1.017: Jesus develops a reputation as a preacher and a healer (Matthew 4:22-35) (Mark 1:39 +) (Luke 4)

In Capernaum, Jesus is reported to have healed a man possessed of an unclean spirit [Luke 4: 31-37] and healed Simon's mother-in-law of a high fever [Luke 4:38-39]. Later he is reported to have similarly cured many who were sick.

Jesus quickly acquired a reputation as a healer. How Jesus healed is a much-debated subject. One traditional view is that Jesus was forgiving ancient sins that were the underlying cause of death (in a sinless world, death is conquered).

[*Today doctors think of viruses, rather than demons, and of psychological illnesses. Does this tell us that Jesus' understanding of the cause of illness was very much of his time and that this shows that he was very human?*]

1.018: The Sermon on the Mount (Matthew 5-7)

It is agreed by many scholars that the sermon may be a summary of Jesus' teaching during his ministry.

His key points: blessed are the poor in spirit and those who mourn, the meek, those who hunger and thirst for righteousness, the merciful, the pure in heart, the peacemakers, and those persecuted for righteousness in Jesus' name.

Note that the Gospel writers indicate that these people will be rewarded in heaven.

[*The emphasis by Jesus is on establishing the right 'mindset' and putting faith into practice – of having the correct attitude and doing right for its own sake, even at risk of persecution.*]

1.019: The Parable of the Salt and Light (Matthew 5: 13-16) (Luke 14:34-35)

This is a cautionary tale about taking care not to lower personal standards. Let your example shine like a light and influence others.

[*Again, the emphasis is upon how one should live and set an example to others, rather simply saying what you believe, or focus on worship. Jesus' preference was for faith in action (doing). Others, he believed, should witness your example.*]

1.020: Jesus and the Law (Matthew 5: 17-20)

Jesus stresses that he does not seek to abolish the Law and that anyone who breaks the least of the Commandments and teaches others to do the same will be the least in the Kingdom of Heaven.

It is difficult to know how to interpret this statement, as Jesus later summed up the Law as being about loving God and your neighbour, implying that this satisfied all the Law and the Prophets.

Hebrew Law is largely concerned with how Jews live their life, which is compatible with Jesus' emphasis on loving your neighbour in an unselfish way, given that God is also your neighbour.

1.021: Jesus on Anger (Matthew 5:21-28) (Luke 12:57-9)

Jesus suggests that before you worship, resolve any quarrels you have with others.

[*This another indicator that Jesus (like John the Baptist) is concerned with repentance and adopting right attitudes and actions outside of the temple, synagogue, or a church. He sees 'doing' and putting his teaching into practice as essential for those who follow believe in him.*]

1.022: Jesus on Adultery (Matthew 5:27-30)

Jesus suggests that adultery starts with initial thoughts or intentions. Getting the mindset right is crucial for his followers.

This idea can be applied to many things besides adultery.

1.023: Jesus on Divorce (Matthew 5:31-32) (Mark 10:11-12) (Luke 16:18)

Jesus indicates that, except on grounds of unchastity, divorce is prohibited (where the husband divorces a wife). If either the husband or wife marries a new partner, they will also be guilty of adultery.

[*This ruling needs to be understood within the context of the ancient world, where divorced women often suffered badly. Jesus' statement was aimed to protect women and restrict the freedom of husbands to get rid of wives often for frivolous reasons.*]

[*This underpins Jesus' concern about how people relate to and love one another.*]

1.024: Jesus on Oaths (Matthew 5:33-37)

Jesus is stressing the need for honesty and commitment and a determination to be a person of your word. Just give your word and mean it. Oaths should be unnecessary.

[This, again, highlights that Jesus was concerned about one's mindset and how it determines what you say or do.]

1.025: Jesus on Retaliation (Matthew 5:38-42)

Jesu rejects the old concept of 'an eye for an eye' and advocates turning the other cheek – thus giving more than you are asked for, giving to beggars, and loans (presumably at zero interest) to those who ask for a loan.

One presumes that this is within one's limits and to a person who is genuinely in need.

[The lesson is that friendship can best be earned by treating deserving people with respect and love. Jesus clearly believes that being indifferent and demanding harsh penalties will promote discord rather than harmony.]

Jesus' thinking here is potentially in conflict with numerous laws being passed by modern democratic governments. Having fixed penalties and zero tolerance very popular when dealing with social problems and is often viewed as the best way to quickly change attitudes.

Arbitration, conciliation, or counselling for differences between people are often dismissed as impractical options, yet they are more in line with Jesus' teaching than fines and prison sentences which may make people feel that they are being treated harshly or being victimized, thus breeding hatred in secret, rather than diminishing it.

1.026: Love your Enemies (Matthew 5:43-48) (Luke 6:27-36)

Jesus rejects violence and suggests that you must learn to love your enemies (by treating them fairly – but maybe only after you have defeated them, in cases where they were genuinely in the wrong?)

Underpinning this advice is the assumption that your enemy can be brought to see you as a friend. (The bully or raw aggressor, or someone who has selfish intensions, may require different tactics to begin with.)

[*I consider that the general treatment of Germans and Japanese after the Second World War were practical applications of Jesus' good advice. The applications healed wounds and promoted long-term harmony.*]

1.027: Charity (Matthew 6:1-4)

Jesus advises people not to make a public scene about giving charitable donations. Do it in secret, he said. Otherwise, public praise is all you will receive.

1.028: Prayer (Matthew 6:5-8)

This is very similar advice to that given about offering alms. *Pray quietly, away from other people. Do not heap up empty phrases like the 'Gentiles' do, "for they think they will be heard because of their many words."*

[*Hence: do not be like some people who pray in synagogues and churches. Or, on street corners, where people may mainly wish to be seen and heard by others?*

It is difficult to read this advice and support much charismatic worship in churches, except when understood as promoting Christian fellowship and training people to focus on Christian attitudes to life.

Having said this, if a person is sincere in advocating charismatic praise of God or Jesus, who am I to judge?]

One accepts that Christians come together in fellowship to reinforce their faith and seek support from other Christians. In this context, many formalized patterns of worship achieve important objectives, especially where what is said has been carefully thought-out.

Jesus stressed his belief that God knows what people need before they ask him. He highlighted the importance of a listening mode in prayer and a need for quiet reflection and meditation to sense what advice God might wish to give.]

[Note: One does not have to have a clear perception of who 'God' is or what he/she/it is like, to believe in the power of prayer.

The key requirement is having 'faith' that prayer 'works' – a firm belief that, through prayer, quiet reflection, and meditation, you will receive answers – a sense of what is the best advice. If the 'voices' in your head are suggesting you should do hateful things, your commonsense should inform you that you are on the wrong wavelength.

Many people now believe that the 'answers' are coming via one's sub-conscious, and not necessarily from 'out there'. One wonders: Is this is how God has always worked?]

1.029: The Lord's Prayer (Matthew 6: 9-15)

Jesus imagined God in a heaven above the skies, as a 'Supreme Being' worthy of human awe and respect. He understood God as active on earth and believed that the food we grow, collect, or prepare, should be seen a gift from God – something that should be received in a spirit of thankfulness.

[It seems good advice to me, even if one is only saying, 'Thank you,' for the provision of food.

Jesus, and John the Baptist, also believed that the kingdom of Heaven would be established on earth very soon, and many of Jesus' followers understood that Jesus' teaching was the first stage in the coming of the expected 'kingdom'.]

Jesus stressed that God should be asked to forgive our sins (our intrinsic human selfishness), but only to the extent that we are prepared to forgive others! This is often forgotten, or still not fully understood by many Christians.

Forgiveness has been advertised by the Christian Church (for centuries) as a prerogative of priests, instead of being something that motivates individual Christians. It has become a 'get-out' clause that reads: 'Do what you like, but make sure you are absolved by a priest before you die.'

Satan was understood by the writers of the gospels as the agent of evil, who was active on earth. The reference in the Lord's Prayer to 'rescue us from the evil one' provided a strong reminder to Christians not to give in to selfish temptations.

[*The Lord's Prayer focusses on how to live our daily life in accordance with the teachings of Jesus. Note that the Lord's Prayer does not necessarily identify any need for clerical assistance or formalized religious practices.*]

1.030: Fasting (Matthew 6:16-18)

As with giving alms and in prayer, followers of Jesus are encouraged to fast in secret. They are encouraged to look their best while they fast and not look glum.

This advice serves to demonstrate that Jesus saw all forms of giving 'worth' to God (i.e.: worship) as potentially cheerful affairs, not to be indulged in to convey the idea that God wants people to live in suffering and misery.

1.031: Treasures on Earth (Matthew 6:19-21)

Many people in the twenty-first century are unimaginably rich in comparison to the minority of the rich elite at the time of Jesus, whose wealth was often built on the misery of others.

Jesus highlights the importance of focusing on spiritual rather than material things.

For much of the history of the Church, this advice has been ignored by leaders of the Church (who often lived like princes). Consequently, many ordinary people may be forgiven for not taking this advice too seriously.

Jesus wished people to understand that being rich in material things does not guarantee happiness. There are too many examples of this fact, in modern newspapers, for this wisdom to be doubted. The lesson is that we all need to share our 'wealth' with others less fortunate than ourselves.

[I am sure that many will agree that doing ordinary things like helping others, is very effective in developing one's spiritual life and enhancing one's peace of mind (especially it is done without any thought of reward, other than personal satisfaction).]

1.032: The Light of the Body (Matthew 6:22-23)

Light in the Bible is equated with good, and darkness with evil. The eye sees the light and spots the correct way to avoid danger. Darkness is associated with blindness and being unable to find the best way, or of being in great danger. Light may also be equated with knowledge and darkness with ignorance.

The ability to *perceive* is a skill that can be developed. It includes the ability to interpret things and is underpinned by having good attitudes. Some see a cup half-full, others a cup half-empty. Some people see problems; others look at the same thing and see opportunities and solutions.

[Jesus' preferred approach to 'seeing' is being able to see the good, not the bad, the opportunities, not the problems. His advice is universal; it applies to everyone, regardless of creed, ethnicity, age, or sexuality.]

1.033: God and Possessions (Matthew 6:24)

This may be linked to Jesus' words on storing up treasures on earth. The two masters are wealth and God.

[It is interesting that this passage refers to a slave and having two masters. In Jesus' day, slavery was practiced in Jewish society as well as in the Roman world. Slavery, then, was a fact of life, and the later Christian assertion that free and slave, male and female are all equal in the sight of God was truly revolutionary. It was as far as any new group could go without risking being immediately destroyed.]

19

1.034: On Anxiety (Matthew 6:25-34)

Jesus suggested that one should not worry about what you will eat or drink, or what to wear, or worry about the future. He said that one should look at the birds, who are fed by the heavenly Father. He also used the example of the lilies of the field and the desires of Gentiles. He stressed that they should strive first for the kingdom of God.

[*Perhaps this is one of those passages that illustrates that Jesus, like John the Baptist, believed that the kingdom of God was imminent. It followed that all normal concerns of human beings were increasingly irrelevant. It is difficult to see this in any other context. In normal life, planning-ahead, sowing and reaping, could make the difference for farmers between survival and starvation.*]

It also suggests that Jesus saw his mission first to his fellow Jews, as he makes disparaging remarks about the Gentiles.

[*Is this also evidence that, at this stage in his ministry, Jesus was truly human and very imperfect in his knowledge? Jesus could not necessarily anticipate how an international religion was going to be forged from his teaching and from his passing.*]

1.035: Judging Others (Matthew 7:1-5)

This is an important example of how Jesus was focusing on how we all live our lives, and on our attitudes. He tells us to be careful about judging people – in case we are later judged by the criteria we use ourselves. He calls us to examine our own practices and recognize our own faults, to discover if we are being hypocritical.

[*This is another example where Jesus' teaching is universal in character and crosses boundaries of time and religion.*]

1.036: Profaning the Holy (Matthew 7:6)

We should not profane the sacred. We will be judged for this, Jesus says.

[Note that nothing in these notes of the Gospels is intended to profane the 'sacred'.]

1.037: Ask, Seek, Knock (Matthew 7:7-11)

Ask and it will be given. Knock and the door will be opened unto you.

[Surely, the assumption here is that this will only apply if your request is reasonable and good in God's eyes?]

1.038: 'Golden Rule' (Matthew 7:12)

Do unto others as you would have them do to you.

[Jesus reinforces this teaching from the Law and the Prophets. It has universal application, regardless of one's philosophy or religion.]

1.040: The Narrow Gate (Matthew 7:13,14)

This focusses on choices made in this life and underpins the idea that few people will be successful in making all the correct choices.

[This supports the view of many Calvinists, at the time of the Reformation, that only the 'elect' will be saved at Final Judgment. Each of the 'elect' was believed to be known to God even before they were born. The rest of the world's population were expected to be condemned to an eternity in hell.

This doesn't build a case for a loving God. This, of course, is a good reason why many Christians now believe that the concept of hell is incompatible with the very idea of there being a loving God.]

Much of Jesus' teaching adopts a loving approach. The Parable of the Good Samaritan and the Parable of the Sheep and the Goats teach that the true measure of a person is the extent to which they are inclined to help those in need, without asking if they will be rewarded for their actions. And in the end, we are told, salvation will be granted through God's grace, rather than because of our own worth.

[*It comes down to whether one either believes in the idea of a God of love, or one believes in the power of God's righteous anger.*]

1.041: The Fruit of Its Tree (Matthew 7:15-20)

Jesus warns about bad prophets, but he suggests that they can be identified by their words. One should ask: Are they promoting harmony or discord, good or bad, hope or despair? It should be obvious, after careful analysis.

1.042: I Never Knew You (Matthew 7:21-23)

This is a warning to those who use the name of God falsely or hypocritically.

1.043: Two House Builders (Matthew 7:24-27)

This follows directly on from above. Jesus warns that his followers should think carefully about his teaching. Those who misunderstand or misinterpret his words will be like someone who builds a house on sand. It will collapse and they will suffer.

[*Given the divisions in the Church over the centuries, some teaching by church leaders must have been in error. As a cleric and friend once said to me, 'We clerics carry a big responsibility; we are accountable.'*]

1.044: The Healing of the Centurion's Servant (Matthew 8:5-13)

This healing is mentioned because it is an example where Jesus healed the servant of a non-Jew: a centurion with faith in the power of Jesus to heal.

Jesus shows that he identifies faith by a person's attitude and acts, and not by a person being an orthodox Jew or a member of any particular sect.

[*Jesus' teaching is universal in practice; it applies potentially to the whole world. You don't need to declare yourself a Christian, though if you do, you will gain in fellowship and be contributing to the future of the Christian Church.*]

1.045: Demon Possessed (Matthew 8:16-17)

This example is referred to because it highlights the way Jesus healed those who were believed to be demon possessed. He was concerned about everyone in need; not simply with good, orthodox Jews.

[*This is consistent with the teaching that God loves everyone: not simply Christians or Jews. There are vast implications here for mission in the twenty-first century.*]

1.046: Would be Followers of Jesus (Matthew 8:18-22)

Jesus refuses the request of someone to take time to bury his father. He adds, 'Let the dead bury their own dead.'

I see this as another example of the extent to which Jesus and John the Baptist saw the kingdom of God as imminent. This meant that normal priorities were to be put to one side, particularly for those who wished to be Jesus' key followers.

[*Would Jesus have said this, had he been aware that the kingdom of God would not have been installed 2000 years after his death?*]

1.047: Healing of a Paralysed Man (Mark 2:1-12)

This example is referred to because it illustrates that when Jesus healed, he believed that he was forgiving the sins that were the underlying cause of much illness and death. He was aware that this was what horrified the Pharisees, as they thought that only God could forgive sins. In their view, Jesus did not have that authority.

[*Today, all physicians speak of viruses and infections. Nobody refers to sin as a cause of illness or death, except in cases of accidents or criminal activity. Is this evidence that Jesus was fully human and far from perfect in his knowledge?*]

1.048: Jesus Calls the Tax Collector (Matthew 9:9-13)

This example is referred to because Jesus makes it clear that his mission is to all who are willing to listen, not simply to healthy, orthodox Jews. He had come to call sinners, not the righteous.

1.049: A Question about Fasting (Matthew 9:14-17)

Jesus seems to suggest here that normal rules about fasting do not apply to his disciples, because he is like the bridegroom at a wedding feast. Then, nobody celebrated while the bridegroom was present; only when he had gone away.

[*Jesus was identifying himself as a very special person in a way that would make his followers see him as a prophet or even as the expected Messiah. Also, as someone who expected to leave them soon.*]

1.050: An Official's Daughter and a Woman's Faith (Matthew 9:18-28)

This is further evidence that Jesus was concerned with all.

Here it is the faith of an 'unclean' women (who had been suffering from bleeding for many years) that Jesus says has healed her.

1.051: The Blind are Healed (Matthew 9:27-31)

A further example of Jesus saying that the faith of sufferers had healed them. Also, it is an example of Jesus warning his followers not to tell others about the healing. One assumes that Jesus did not want to draw too much attention to himself at this point in his mission.

[*As John the Baptist had shown, it was dangerous to make enemies of people in authority. They could act quickly against you.*]

1.052: Coming Persecutions (Matthew 10:17-39)

Jesus warns his key disciples that they will face persecution, and he promises them that he will acknowledge their courage to his Father in heaven.

Given the evidence of the arrest of John the Baptist and of opposition from some Pharisees, Jesus was pointing out the obvious, and providing needed moral support to his close disciples.

[*Jesus recognized that his cause would divide families, and in some instances, disciples would have to choose between loyalty to Jesus or to their parents.*]

1.053: John the Baptist in Prison (Matthew 11:2-19)

Jesus' message to John in prison is to tell him that the blind will see, the lame walk, lepers are healed, the deaf will hear, the dead are raised, and the poor will hear good news.

[*This was consistent with the reputation that Jesus was gaining as a healer, a miracle worker, a teacher, and possibly as the expected Messiah.*]

Others were not impressed and accused Jesus of being a glutton, a drunkard, and a friend of tax collectors and sinners.

[*This, at least, confirms that Jesus was popular with many people and that he was prepared to celebrate with people and speak to the unclean and to sinners. It also appears that Jesus believed that being cheerful was a good thing.*]

1.054: Unbelieving Towns (Matthew 11:25-27)

These are words spoken by Jesus in bitterness, it seems, because towns like Capernaum had not received his teaching and repented. Jesus suggests that Capernaum will suffer worse than Sodom on the Day of Judgment.

[*Were these really the words of Jesus? If they are, they portray him as a perfectly normal human being, prone to disappointment, anger, and of him making threats that he might later regret.*]

There are several instances in the Gospels where one senses that the Gospel writers are remembering what happened to Jesus, and they wished to illustrate what they imagined as Jesus' anger and frustration. These instances require careful study. They can portray Jesus as a very normal human being.

1.055: Thanks to his Father (Matthew 11:25-27)

This continues in the same vein as above, revealing Jesus in a despondent mood.

[*Jesus' references to his Father are that of a subordinate. What does this tell us about the nature of the Trinity?*]

1.056: Come to Me and Rest (Matthew 11:28-30)

And then a complete change of tone! 'Come to me all who are weary and are carrying heavy burdens, and I will give you rest. Take my yoke upon you and learn from me. For I am humble and gentle in heart, and you will find rest for your souls. For my yoke is easy, and my burden is light.'

[*This is Jesus talking to the crowds, rather than to his disciples, indicating that he sees his teaching as easy to accept by those who understand where he is coming from. These are people who have empathy with Jesus' call to love your neighbour as yourself and help others when you can. The burden is light for those who have the same mindset and motivation as Jesus.]*

1.057: Working on the Sabbath (Matthew 12:1-8)

This conclusion is in Mark 2 (vs 27): The sabbath was made for humankind, and not humankind for the sabbath.

Also: The Son of Man (Jesus) is Lord of the sabbath.

[Jesus gives examples where priests break the sabbath in the temple, but maybe his main point is his claim to have authority to decide what is appropriate on the sabbath: this is a claim that would have shocked many of his hearers.]

1.058: The Man with the Paralysed Hand (Matthew 12:9-14)

This occurs in a synagogue on the sabbath, in the presence of shocked Pharisees, as presumably Jesus knew it would. He also knew that it would make them want to destroy him.

[Was Jesus deliberately provoking them?]

1.059: Here is My Servant (Matthew 12:15-21)

The point here is that it was prophesied in Isaiah that many of those healed would be Gentiles.

Jesus was acknowledged as 'The Son of God', but Jesus ordered everyone not to tell this to others.

[This does beg the question of how Jews, generally, can be accused of rejecting Jesus as the Son of God, when most of them were never told this might be the case?]

1.060: At the Home of a Pharisee (Luke 7:36-50)

Jesus eats with a Pharisee. A woman who is described as a sinner enters the house and anoints Jesus' feet with an expensive ointment.

[*Jesus praised the woman's action and faith, and he forgives her sins. This angered many Pharisees because they assumed that Jesus did not have the authority to forgive sins. Only God could do this.*]

1.061: Women with Jesus (Luke 8:1-3)

Jesus preaches in many places accompanied by the twelve disciples and women: including Mary Magdalene (from whom seven demons had gone out), Joanna (wife of Herod's steward, Chuza), Susanna and others.

[*These women provided for them out of their 'own resources'.*]

1.062: Jesus' Mothers and Brothers (Matthew 12:46-50)

Jesus is preaching in a house, when his mother and brothers come outside and ask for him. Jesus asks who they are, and he suggests that all who do the will of his Father in heaven are family to him – they are also his mother, sisters, and brothers.

Given the strength of ties associated with the family in Jesus' days, this incident must have shocked many readers, or people who heard the story.

[*This illustrates Jesus' sense of the importance of his supporters identifying themselves as his 'family', in the urgency of the coming kingdom of heaven.*]

1.063: Parable of the Sower (Matthew 13:1-8) (Mark:4: 1-9) (Luke 8:4-8)

The Sower's seeds fell on the path and were eaten by birds, or on rocky ground with little soil where they grew quickly; then they died, scorched in the sun among thorns that choked them; other seeds fell on good soil and brought forth grain, in varying degrees of abundance.

[*The parallel is the teaching of Jesus. Some people do not understand because it is too sophisticated, or they do not listen. By contrast, those who have ears to hear, they understand the parable: they are the good 'soil', and they will spread the word.*]

1.064: Speaking in Parables (Matthew 13:10-18) (Mark 4:10-12) (Luke 8:9-10)

The authors of the Gospels give their own views on why Jesus spoke in parables.

[*I like to think that Jesus taught in parables because he respected people. He believed they were able to work out the meaning of any parable – and having done so, they would better grasp and remember the thinking underlying the story. Jesus was not simply telling people the 'right' answer, he was expecting them to think and to learn. Surely, this is an argument, today, for having less 'preaching' and more 'teaching'?*]

1.065: Interpretation of the Parable of the Sower (Matthew 13:18-23) (Mark 4:13-20) (Luke 8:11-15)

[*Are these later additions to the Gospels, to clarify Jesus' words? They make the stories rather boring.*]

1.066: The Parable of the Growing Seed (Mark 4:26-29)

This parable compares the secret growth of seed with the hidden development of spiritual knowledge. The harvesting at the end of the process hints at Final Judgment.

1.067: The Parable of the Weeds (Matthew 13:24-30)

This develops the same theme as above, implying that the weeds equate to sinners, who will burn in hell.

This parable is explained in Matthew 13:36-43.

[*Is this another later modification of the Gospel, and strictly unnecessary?*]

Matthew writes that, at the end of the age, the Son of Man will send his angels, who will throw sinners into the furnace of hell.

[*Did Jesus believe this will happen? Do we believe this will happen? Or is this another example of the Gospel writers saying what they think Jesus should have said? Each one of us needs to decide for ourselves.*]

1.068: The Parable of the Mustard Seed
(Matthew 13:31-32) (Mark 4:30-32) (See Luke 13:18,19)

This likens the development of Judaism and Christianity to the slow growth of the Mustard Tree, or to the slow spiritual growth of many an individual.

1.069: The Parables of the Hidden Treasure and
the Pearl (Mark 4:35-41) (Luke 8:22-25)

The hidden treasure and the valuable pearl equate to the kingdom of heaven.

1.070: The Parable of the Net (Matthew 13:47-50)

At Final Judgment all will be gathered: the good will be saved and the bad thrown away.

[*Many Christians still believe in Final Judgment.*

I would have thought that it would be far easier for God to grant eternal life only to those who have earned it and allow everybody else to die naturally. Making the rest suffer tortures in hell for eternity will require a great deal of organizing. Is the devil up to it?

I have always valued the concept of Final Judgment. The very idea provides a litmus test for anybody to reflect on a thought, or on something they have said, or something they have done. How would it be judged at Final Judgment? Do you regret the thought, the words, or the action? Did they hurt somebody? If you are a moral person, you will dislike the idea of letting yourself down and amend your thinking, saying, or doing.]

1.071: Jesus Calms the Storm (Mark 4:35-41) (Luke 8:22-25)

The *New Bible Commentary*, page 958, suggests that we do not know how Jesus performs miracles and expresses a further view that we *do not need to know.*

[*Did the storm die away, and the event became more dramatic in subsequent repetitions of the tale?*]

[*Those who believe in the supernatural will wish to stress the extent to which Jesus was showing his authority over natural forces. Those who are skeptical will focus on the fact that something happened that impressed the disciples, sufficient for it to be recorded.*]

[*When we die, if the story is factual, we shall find out. But I wonder: Is God bothered, one way or another? What matters, surely, is that we appreciate the lesson in the tale.*]

1.072: A Man with Demons (Mark 5:1-20) (Luke 8:26-39)

The man healed is an outsider and 'unclean', and this is a key point to note. Jesus was prepared to heal him.

Modern readers may have sympathy for the two thousand swine, after Jesus is reported to have told several demons to leave the demon-infested man and enter the animals. The swine are reported to have panicked and rushed down a steep bank into the sea, where they drowned.

[*Today, trained doctors and nurses, world-wide, do not imagine mentally ill people as 'demon-possessed'.*]

One can only hope that there is a 'modern' way of telling this story that highlights how Jesus' reputation as a healer spread wherever he went.

[*More than anything, suggesting that Jesus exorcised demons when healing people, confirms that Jesus was very human and only understood the world and medicine in the same way as his contemporaries.*]

1.073: Jesus is Rejected at Nazareth
(Matthew 13:53-58) (Mark 6:1-6a)

Jesus shocked people in his hometown by his claims.

[*Jesus is called the 'son of Mary' (not the son of Joseph). This may indicate that, locally, Jesus' parentage had long been questioned.*]

His brothers are named as James, Joses, Judas, and Simon, and his sisters are said to have been present.

Jesus was said to be amazed at the unbelief; yet he acknowledged that prophets are not generally honoured in their hometown.

[*This passage provides a believable image of Jesus, as a real and ordinary person, well-known in Nazareth. They knew what he had been like as a young boy.*]

1.074: Jesus Feeds Five Thousand
(Mark 6:30 -44)

People in past centuries expected miracles and accepted this story as factual. Today, many people see it as a 'big-fish' story, where the details may have been exaggerated in successive versions of the story. However, others are still prepared to accept it as accurate and 'God-breathed'.

[*The story confirms Jesus' high reputation as a teacher. The food provided symbolizes spiritual 'food' that Jesus offered in overflowing abundance.*]

1.075: Jesus Walks on the Water (Matthew 14:22-33) (Mark 6:45-52)

[Did Jesus walk out in shallow water on a sandbank? Or is the story factual? Each reader must decide for themselves. To Christians over centuries, it illustrates the authority of Jesus as the son of God.]

1.076: Healings at Gennesaret (Matthew 14:34-36) (Mark 6:53-56)

Jesus healed many people, including those who touched his cloak.

As noted above, for Christians over centuries, the story illustrated the divinity and authority of Jesus as the Son of God.

Kings have since often wondered whether they also had a little of this same power to heal people.

1.077: Things that Make a Person Unclean (Matthew 15:1-20) (Mark 7:1-23)

This is an interesting reflection on 'tradition' as essential to underpin modern practice: for example: washing hands before eating. Jesus concludes that it is not what goes into the mouth that defiles a person, but what comes out of person.

[In Jesus' day, no one thought about infections and viruses and how they might be transmitted. What does this say about Jesus' level of knowledge?]

Given the logic of the time, Jesus argued that it was what came out of human that was unclean, not what went in. He was thinking of bad language and ideas and unsound religious theories: things that come from the human 'heart' – evil intentions, fornication, theft, murder, avarice, wickedness, deceit, licentiousness, envy, slander, pride, folly.

[*Jesus was teaching the importance of having a right mindset, with good intentions and a wish to help others.*]

1.078: A Woman's Faith (Matthew 15:21-28) (Mark 7:24-30)

This is a key passage that tells us much about Jesus' mission.

In the district of Tyre and Sidon, a Canaanite woman approached Jesus on behalf of her sick daughter.

Jesus refused to answer her, and his disciples attempted to persuade him to send her away.

Jesus said, 'I was only sent to the lost sheep of the house of Israel' and later added, 'It is not fair to take the children's food and throw it to the dogs.' [*Was Jesus hoping, simply, to shock the woman?*]

The woman challenged Jesus with, 'Yes, Lord, yet even the dogs eat crumbs that fall from their master's table.'

Jesus was impressed. He praised the woman's faith and told her that her daughter was healed.

Here, Jesus responded positively to a foreigner and a woman. Initially, he was inclined to dismiss her, then seemed to change his mind.

[*This story has implications regarding the extent to which Jesus was perfect. It also seems to confirm that his mission was to all: Jew, non-Jew; Christian; non-Christian.*]

1.079: Jesus Heals many People (Matthew 15:29-31) (Mark 7:31-37)

Near the Sea of Galilee, Jesus healed the lame, the maimed, the blind, the mute and the deaf.

Jesus was gaining a solid reputation as a healer. Many understand this as evidence of his power to forgive the underlying sins that were believed to cause illness and death, and evidence of the power of the God of Israel.

[How Jesus healed and the extent to which the cures were miraculous is open to discussion. People believe what they believe.]

1.080: Jesus Feeds Four Thousand. (Matthew 15:32-39) (Mark 8:1-10)

Seven loaves and a few small fish were sufficient to feed four thousand people.

Is this a genuine miracle or evidence of a story being made more fantastical with each re-telling?

[Do all people have to believe it today? – except as evidence of Jesus' growing reputation.]

1.081: Demand for a Miracle (Matthew 16:1-4) (Mark 8:11-13)

When some Pharisees demand a sign, Jesus' view seems to have been that the mere fact that they were all living in an 'evil and adulterous generation' was sign enough from heaven that things needed to change urgently.

1.082: The Yeast of the Pharisees and Sadducees (Matthew 16:5-12) (Mark 8:14-21)

Jesus warns his disciples that he is more concerned about the teachings of the Pharisees and the Sadducees than he is about shortages of food.

1.083: The Blind Man of Bethsaida (Mark 8:22-26)

Jesus is believed to have restored the man's sight by laying his hands upon his eyes.

1.084: The Confession at Caesarea Philippi (Matthew 16:13-23) (Mark 8:27-33) (Luke 9:18-22)

Simon Peter says that he believes Jesus is the Messiah.

Jesus then tells Peter that he (Peter) is the rock on which Jesus will build his church. He adds that he is giving Peter the keys to the kingdom of heaven and all the authority that goes with them. [*This, of course, is the basis of the theory of 'apostolic succession'.*]

The difficulty is knowing whether these passages are original or are additions that were included to strengthen the authority of the early Roman Catholic Church.

[*Is it justifiable that authority can be handed down forever to future church leaders, when no one can know in advance whether the next leader will be competent or incompetent, a saint, or a hypocrite?*]

Again, Jesus told the disciples to keep secret the fact that he was the Messiah. One can understand the dangers of his enemies discovering this, but had the disciples kept this secret, few people would ever have known that Jesus was any more than a good teacher and healer.

[*Given this situation: How could the Jews, collectively, have ever been accused of killing the Son of Man or the Son of God?*]

The above passages end with Jesus warning his disciples that he will go to Jerusalem and by killed and he will rise again on the third day.

[*Is this another example passage where the Gospel writer added words to show that Jesus could foretell the future?*

Is it more likely that Jesus often talked about the risks he knew he would run in Jerusalem, where he had many enemies at the highest social level? He didn't need to be perfect to work out that he might be killed there.

It seems that Jesus was determined to go to Jerusalem, and he also seems to have expected to die there.

Did he expect to be murdered by his enemies, or even be stoned to death? Surely, the last thing he may have expected is to be handed to the Romans to be crucified?]

1.085: Conditions of Discipleship (Matthew 16:24-28) (Mark 8:34 – 9: 1) (Luke 9:23-27)

Jesus predicts future suffering for his disciples and is reported to have said that they should, 'take up their cross'. This implies that he knew for certain that he would be crucified, which is unlikely. Some scholars believe that this reference to the 'cross' reflects the later knowledge by the Gospel authors of what had happened to Jesus.

Of great importance in this passage in Mark is the clear statement of Jesus' belief that '. . . *there are some standing here who will not taste death until they see that the kingdom of God has come with power.*'

[*It is a historical fact that this did not happen on earth, though many of Jesus' followers and even St Paul probably expected it to happen imminently. Does this indicate that Jesus' knowledge of the future was far from perfect?*]

1.086: The Transfiguration (Matthew 17:1-8) (Mark 9:2-8) (Luke 9:28-36)

Jesus went up a mountain to pray, taking Peter, James, and John.

There he was 'transfigured' (His face shone like the sun and his clothes were dazzling white). Moses and Elijah were reported to have appeared with Jesus. A voice from the heavens is also reported to have said, 'This is my Son, my Chosen, listen to him.'

Many Christians believe this happened exactly as it is written in the Gospel, but increasingly people may understand this as a literary device designed to impress future generations that Jesus was approved by Moses and Elijah. Such supernatural appearances are today seen as reflecting ancient superstitions.

[*My instinct is to believe that if something like this happened 2000 years ago, there is no reason why something similar could not happen in 2022. What also makes me uneasy is that the witnesses 'kept silent and in those days told no one of the things they had seen.'*]

As they came down from the mountain, Jesus complicated matters, by suggesting to them that *'Elijah has already come, but they did not recognize him.'*

[*What did the disciples make of that? Was Jesus saying that he was Elijah?*]

The story of the Transfiguration raises more questions than it provides answers.

1.087: Jesus Speaks about His Death (Matthew 17:22-23) (Mark 9:30-32) (Luke 9:43b-45)

The words are: 'The Son of man is going to be betrayed into human hands, and they will kill him, and on the third day, he will be raised.'

It is suggested that the disciples were too afraid to ask Jesus further questions about this.

1.088: Who is the Greatest? (Matthew 18:1-5) (Mark 9:33-37) (Luke 9:46-48)

Jesus: 'Unless you change and become like children, you will never enter the kingdom of heaven.'

This teaches the need for humility. 'The greatest among you will be their servant' (Matthew 23:11). 'All who exalt themselves will be humbled and those who humble themselves will be exalted.' (Matthew 23:12)

[*The theme is the 'Servant King'; the idea that Jesus' life was one of service to others and that part of the life of a follower of Jesus should be service to others, regardless of their rank. It is linked to the idea that in heaven the great will not lord it over everybody.*]

1.089: Who is for us? (Mark 9:38-41) (Luke 9:49-50)

The disciples tell Jesus they have seen someone healing people in Jesus' name. Jesus answers: 'Whoever is not against us is for us.'

The idea is that no one has a monopoly of the work of the kingdom.

[*This may be interpreted that anyone who does good work is doing it for Jesus, whether he or she knows it or not, as in the Parable of the Sheep and the Goats – about Final Judgment.*]

Jesus warns that anyone putting a stumbling block that stops others following Jesus will suffer the consequences. (Mark 9:42-49)

1.090: The Parable of the Lost Sheep
(Matthew 18:10-14)

Jesus warms to the theme of a shepherd rejoicing to find a lost sheep. ('There is more joy in heaven over one sinner who repents than over ninety-nine persons who need no repentance.')

One can understand this but understand why all others may not all be sympathetic here.

1.091: On Reproving Another Believer
(Matthew 15:18-20)

[*One can't help feeling that this passage is addressing problems found in the early church and that Jesus' teaching and words are being tweaked to deal with these later problems.*]

The advice is that problems raised should be handled carefully and if the person needs to be reproved, then it should be done in a way that encourages the offender to repent and be forgiven.

1.092: Forgiveness (Matthew 18:21-22)
(Luke 17:4)

Peter asks Jesus how many times a member of the church should be allowed to sin against him and be forgiveness. Jesus' answer of 'seventy-seven' times seems to imply 'as many times as is necessary'.

Of some concern here is the use of the word 'church', which had no direct application while Jesus was alive – except as meaning a 'community' of believers. This suggests that the Gospel is being written to send messages to the early Christian churches.

[*This passage is important because there is little evidence that the later Christian Church had much sympathy with the spirit of Jesus' teaching on forgiveness. Later, forgiveness was adopted as a prerogative of the clergy to use. It became something that could be withheld, as easily as it could be granted.*]

The passage is also important because it is at odds with much law-making in the modern Western world. Punishment and fixed penalties are often preferred, even when there is evidence of genuine repentance. Making an example of someone is popular; forgiving them is not.

1.093: The Parable of the Unmerciful Servant
(Matthew 18:23-25)

Jesus uses this parable to emphasize the importance of forgiving people who are genuinely repentant.

The message is that if we do not forgive others, we should not expect to be forgiven for our own transgressions. This is a fundamental requirement for any person who follows the teaching of Jesus. It is not a popular approach in Western society in the twenty-first century.

1.094: Sending out of the Seventy (Matthew 9:37-38) (Luke 10:1-16)

It is difficult to accept that these are the accurate words of Jesus as they are in complete conflict with Matthew 18:21-22 above on forgiveness.

This passage includes dire warnings of even worse punishments than those suffered by Sodom and Gomorrah. The passage seems to be more concerned with confirming the future powers of clerics than about Jesus' teaching.

1.095: The Return of the Seventy (Luke 10:17-20)

[*I cannot imagine Jesus saying, 'I watched Satan fall from heaven like a flash of lightning. See, I have given you power to tread on snakes and scorpions . . . and nothing will hurt you.' It does not match reality. If there is error, it must be in the way Jesus' words were recorded.*]

1.096: Jesus Rejoices (Luke 10:21-22)

Jesus says he is glad that his words are hidden from the wise and intelligent but they are understood by infants.

[*This is surely the writer of the Gospel imagining what Jesus might have said. There is no love in the content of these words.*]

1.097: The Greatest Commandment (Matthew 22:34-40) (Mark 12:28-31) (Luke 10:25-28)

All the Synoptic Gospels agree that Jesus said the words: 'You should love God with all our strength and mind and your neighbour as yourself.'

[*If we imagine God as our neighbour, this is reduced to a single commandment.*]

1.098: The Parable of the Good Samaritan (Luke 10:29-37)

The moral of this parable is that goodness can be identified in anybody – by their motivation and their words or actions, and it should be recognized for what it is.

[*The implication is that goodness is nothing to do with a person calling themselves a Jew, a Christian, a Muslim, or an atheist.*]

The Good Samaritan demonstrates that he loves his neighbour by his act of helping a stranger in need. It is real worship in practice. He does not need to declare that he is doing it in the name of Jesus; what matters is that he does it. He has the mindset of Jesus and the blessing of God.

[*This parable has major implications for Christianity in the twenty-first century, operating in a multicultural world.*]

1.099: Martha and Mary (Luke 10:38-42)

The importance of this story is that is makes clear that seeking spiritual enhancement is as equally applicable to women as it is to men. [*It is another example of Jesus' teaching being universal in character.*]

1.100: The Return of the Evil Spirit (Luke 11:24-28)

These reported words of Jesus reflect the mindset of his age regarding illness. Illness was often attributed to demons or evil spirits.

Jesus is reported to have said: 'When an unclean spirit has gone out of a person, it wanders through waterless regions looking or a resting place, but not finding any, it says, "I will return to my house from which I came." When it comes, it finds it swept and put in order. Then it goes and brings seven other spirits, more evil than itself, and they enter and live there . . .'

[*One presumes that the author of the Gospel believed that Jesus had said these words, or he is using the example to demonstrate the knowledge and power of Jesus. Either way, the example is rendered worthless in the light of modern ideas about the causes of illness. If Jesus said these words, they prove that his knowledge was far from perfect.*]

1.101: Exhortation to Fearless Confession (Luke 12:2-12)

An interesting distinction is made here between someone denying the 'Son of Man' when they are ignorant of who is the Son of Man, and those who deny the Son of Man while knowing full well it is Jesus. It teaches that anyone who denies the working of the Holy Spirit in Jesus (for example by suggesting he is controlled by Satan) will be judged harshly.

It is notable that Jesus often told his disciples to keep secret who he was. It follows that most people were ignorant that his disciples believed that it was the Holy Spirit operating in Jesus.

[*These warnings do not seem to me to reflect the normal forgiving nature of Jesus.*]

1.102: The Parable of the Rich Fool (Luke 12:13-21)

Jesus warns against being like the rich man, who built large barns to store his surplus grain for the future, because life is not all about material things and possessions. He may be dead next day or be robbed.

[*Jesus emphasized getting the spirit life right as a priority, but he was speaking in the declared expectation of the imminent coming of the kingdom of God, which did not happen in the way he and many early Christians expected it to happen. This was the context of Jesus' world. In normal daily life, of course, building large barns to hold grain for future periods of drought or for one's family, may be sound practice.*]

1.103: On Anxiety (Matthew 6:25-33) (Luke 12:22-34)

This develops the theme of the Parable of the Rich Fool. Jesus believed he was playing a key part in establishing the imminent kingdom of God on earth. His advice was to think of today, rather than about tomorrow, and follow the example of the birds and the plants.

[*Like John the Baptist, Jesus believed that there was an urgent reason to focus on developing spiritual values and on repentance.*

This explains why some of Jesus' advice appears to turn on its head normal thinking about planning for the future as best practice.]

1.104: Watchfulness and Faithfulness (Matthew 24:43-51) (Luke 12:35-46)

This continues the theme of being ready, now, for the imminent kingdom of God. The writer of the Gospel is happy to use images of the duty of a slave to serve master with diligence, even if the master is away.

[*Slavery was a fact of life in Roman times – no individual group could do anything about it.*]

1.105: No Peace, but a Sword (Matthew 10:34-36) (Luke 12:49-56)

This is not the best example of Jesus' teaching but, nonetheless, it reflects a truth. Becoming a dedicated disciple of Jesus involved great risks. Many people would be against you and there could easily be divisions in families, like in a civil war.

[*This was not the aim of Jesus' teaching but, given human nature, it was a likely outcome in certain cases.*]

1.106: Settling Quarrels (Matthew 5:25-26) (Luke 12:57-59)

This is a theme in the New Testament. Jesus' followers and early Christians were advised to settle all quarrels with others before going to the synagogue, the Temple, or to a 'church' to worship God.

[*It is also good advice today. Settle any quarrels with others amicably while you can. If you allow lawyers, magistrates, or judges to get involved, you will deeply regret it.*]

1.107: Turn from Your Sins or Die
(Luke 13:1-9)

This passage emphasises Jesus' belief that the Jewish nation needed to focus urgently on repentance of their sins – because the kingdom of heaven was imminent. The fruit tree is believed to symbolize Israel: a tree that normally required at least three years before it produced figs.

1.108: Jesus Heals a Crippled Woman (Luke 13:10-17)

Jesus is criticized for healing a sick woman in the synagogue on the sabbath. He gives examples to show that in cases of need, healing or helping should be done immediately, regardless of the day.

1.109: The Parables of the Mustard Seed and
the Yeast (Matthew 13:31-33) (Mark 4:30-32)
(Luke 13:18-21)

These are images of the kingdom of God: as a mustard seed that grows into a large tree, or as yeast that is used in making bread.

1.110: The Narrow Door (Matthew 7:13-14)
(Mark 10:31) (Luke 13:22-30)

Not the most encouraging passage in the Gospels. The way to eternal salvation is likened to a narrow door, where large numbers of people are pushing and shoving to get through.

1.111: The Departure from Galilee (Luke 13:31-33)

Jesus indicates that he will be going to Jerusalem for 'it is impossible for a prophet to be killed outside of Jerusalem.'

[*This indicates that he saw himself as a prophet and expected to die in Jerusalem.*]

1.112: Jesus' Love for Jerusalem (Matthew 23:37-39) (Luke 13:34-35)

This seems to indicate that when Jesus enters Jerusalem the people will be ready to welcome him, in the name of the Lord.

1.113: Healing of the Man with Dropsy (Luke 14:1-6)

This is another example, where Jesus heals on the sabbath.

1.114: Teaching on Humility (Luke 14:7-14)

Jesus taught the need for humility and here gives two examples.

First: sitting in the lowest place when you are invited as a guest. Second: when you hold a banquet, invite the poor, the crippled, the lame, and the blind. You will be blessed because they cannot repay you.

[*It follows that all Christians should seek to be humble when dealing with others.*]

The history of Christianity demonstrates that Church leaders have failed miserably in this regard. From the beginning, leaders have arisen who have no patience with anybody's views than their own, and the idea of 'Apostolic Succession' has been used to impose a top-down dictatorship throughout the centuries.

Key leaders, at the time of the Reformation, adopted the same approach: their view was that everybody else was wrong. And even in the last centuries Christians have often refused to respect other religions, dismissing them as 'pagan'.

[In the multi-cultural world of the twenty-first century, all Christians need to re-visit Jesus' emphasis on the need for humility, starting with an awareness that one's own individual interpretation of the Bible is limited by huge cultural and historical blinkers that restrict one's vision and hearing.

The suggestion is that we must all start to be genuinely interested in the views of others, to discover shared ideas, and how much we can learn from our neighbour.]

1.115: The Parable of the Wedding Feast (Matthew 22:1-10) (Luke 14:15-24)

The theme is that God invites people who have no standing in society (such as the tax-collectors, unclean people, outsiders, and the other 'sinners').

1.116: The Cost of Discipleship (Matthew 10:37-38) (Luke: 14:25-35)

[This has the whiff of authors of the Gospel, who were interpreting Jesus' thoughts in the light of their own later knowledge of the life and death of Jesus and of the Crucifixion.

Did Jesus think that his disciples should hate their own parents? Or did he explain that discipleship could often involve tensions with family members and the need for them to make difficult choices, and include giving up all possessions?]

1.117: The Parables of the Sheep and the Lost Coin (Matthew 18:12-24) (Luke 15:1-10)

This is a recurrent theme in the Gospels. Jesus has come to save sinners and it is natural for someone to rejoice greatly when a lost sheep or a lost coin is found after a long search. The other 'sheep' do not always accept this rejoicing, and other family members and helpers may often feel ignored.

1.118: The Parable of the Prodigal Son (Luke 15:11-32)

This is very the well-known story that illustrates the above idea about lost and found. It highlights the importance of forgiveness in Christian living.

Note that the brother called one of their 'slaves' to ask what the celebrations were about. He was angry to discover that his father was rejoicing because his prodigal son had returned.

[*The story shows how difficult this sort of generosity can be for others to accept, when their loyalty seems to have been taken for granted. One needs to adopt willingly the mindset of the 'shepherd' and empathize with the joy that he or she feels, when one of the flock is found, after having been 'lost'.*]

1.119: The Unjust Manager (Luke 16:1-13)

The moral of this story is disputed. It is not easy to make sense of it.

1.120: About the Law and Divorce (Matthew 11:12-13) (Luke 16:16-19)

The teaching is that a man who divorces his wife (except on grounds of unchastity) and marries another commits adultery, and a man who marries a divorced women also commits adultery.

[*This must be linked to other statements by Jesus on divorce where it becomes clearer that Jesus was protecting women in this period, from a husband who wished to put aside his wife for frivolous reasons, thus leaving the wife in difficult financial circumstances where she could starve or be forced into prostitution.*]

1.121: The Rich Man and Lazarus (Luke 16:19-31)

There is an intriguing comment: 'If they do not listen to Moses and the prophets, neither may they be convinced even if someone rises from the dead.'

The central message here is that, in this life, one should believe in the Law and seek to help those who are less fortunate than yourself. It is too late after death. *[One imagines that the Gospel author sees Jesus referring to his own end and thinking that some people will refuse to listen to anybody!]*

1.122: Temptations to Sin (Matthew 18:6-7) (Mark 9:42) (Luke 17:1-2)

This another passage which emphasizes that Final Judgment is concerned with how you live your life and treat other people. Or it is warning about procuring and grooming young people, so that they fall into evil ways: this is identified as a serious sin. *[As Ghislaine Maxwell has recently discovered, to perhaps an excessive cost?]*

1.123: On the Power of Faith (Matthew 17:20) (Luke 17:5-6)

Jesus says that if you have enough faith, it will move mountains. Or, with enough faith, you could say to a mulberry tree 'be uprooted and planted in the sea, and it would obey.'
[The authors of the Gospels may be using hyperbole to underpin the importance of faith. If they are being literal, it implies that supernatural forces can be invoked by the words of believers. In past centuries, this sort of thing was accepted willingly. But can one accept this suggestion in 2022?]

1.124: The Slave's Wages (Luke 17:7-10)

This illustrates the world in which Jesus lived and the ordinariness of slavery. The slave is owed no thanks for doing a job well.
[Is Luke suggesting that we are to understand ourselves as worthless slaves who are doing only what we ought to do?

I should hope not. Surely, anybody who does a good job is worthy of thanks.]

1.125: The Healing of Ten Lepers (Luke 17:11-19)

This is another example that illustrates Jesus' view that it is not who you are that counts, but what you think, say, and do. The only one of the ten lepers who thinks of saying, 'Thank you' to Jesus is a Samaritan – a foreigner in the eyes of orthodox Jews.

[*To us the Samaritan is the equivalent of somebody who is not a Christian.*]

[*This demonstrates that Jesus' teaching was universal in character. Even if Jesus was preaching mainly to Jews and for Jews, his teaching has potential application to benefit everybody.*]

1.126: The Kingdom of God (Luke 17:20-21)

Jesus said that the kingdom of God is not coming with things that can be observed, so that you can say, 'Here it is.' He added that it is here already.

[*Many commentators interpret this to mean that Jesus' life on earth was a first stage in the arrival of the kingdom of God/ kingdom of heaven.*]

1.127: The Coming of the Son of Man (Matthew 24:26-28) (Luke 17:22-37)

The day of the Son of Man is believed to refer to the Second Coming, or immediately before Jesus' 'Second Coming'. It is suggested that there will be no signs in advance, and only those who have stopped thinking solely of themselves will be saved.

[*It presents a grim picture for many, and for this reason, it appears to be the sort of thing that the Gospel writers may*

*have wished to highlight, to make people afraid of not being
ready for Final Judgment.*

*There is nothing here of the positive imagery associated
with Jesus' principal teaching on earth.*]

1.128: The Parable of the Widow and the Judge (Luke 18:1-8)

The theme here is the persistence of the petitioner. A parallel is
found in those who pray, 'Thy kingdom come,' to God, hoping
it will eventually arrive.

Luke affirms that God will honour this prayer at the
appropriate time, with the return of Jesus.

The message is that if you believe you are right, keep at it.
Eventually, you will be heard.

1.129: The Parable of the Pharisee and the Tax Collector (Luke 18:9-14)

These men went to the Temple to pray. The Pharisee exalted
himself and identified the things he had done. The Tax
Collector confessed that he was a sinner and asked for God's
mercy.

Jesus declared that all who exalt themselves will be humbled
and all who humble themselves will be exalted.

[*Note that the Tax Collector was a sinner in the eyes of
Jesus' contemporaries. Today, he could be a non-Christian.*]

THE JUDEAN SECTION

Matthew 19-27; Mark 10; Luke 18: 15 to 23.26

1.130: On Marriage and Divorce (Matthew 19:1-12) (Mark 10:1-12)

This has been referred to earlier.

Jesus says, 'what God has joined together, let no one separate.' 'Whoever divorces him wife, except for unchastity, and marries another commits adultery. And if she divorces her husband and marries another, she commits adultery.'

[*Recent commentators have suggested that this ruling was intended to benefit wives from being discarded for frivolous reasons and being left to starve or become prostitutes. It was there to challenge men and help women. Is this an example of values that can be adapted to suit recent thinking?*]

1.131: Jesus Blesses Children (Matthew 19:13-15) (Mark 10:13-16) (Luke 18:15-17)

Children accept teaching uncritically. Jesus suggests that this is the secret in accepting his teaching.

1.132: The Rich Man (Matthew 19:16-30) (Mark 10:17-31) (Luke 15:18-30)

This parable leads to Jesus saying, 'It is easier for a camel to go through the eye of a needle than for someone who is rich to enter the kingdom of God.' The key idea here is that anything is possible with God's grace.

Jesus identifies key commandments as: You shall not murder; you shall not commit adultery; you shall not steal; you shall not bear false witness; honor your mother and father; and love your neighbor as yourself. The rich man says he has observed all these commandments.

The apostles and all who have left families and possessions to follow Jesus were disappointed at this point, and Jesus indicated that they will be rewarded in heaven.

[*Note: This needs to be linked to Jesus' parable of the Sheep and the Goats, where people who help others for no reward and no awareness of Jesus are promised salvation.*]

1.133: The Parable of the Labourers in the Vineyard (Matthew 20:1-16)

Workers all received the same daily wages regardless of the number of hours they had work and some grumbled, despite having agreed to the employer's terms.

[*The key idea here is that in heaven, 'the last will be first and the first will be last.' The suggestion is that this is not based on human ideas of fairness but on God's grace which is granted to each person as God wills.*]

1.134: Jesus Speaks a Third Time about His Death (Matthew 20:17-19) (Mark 10:32-34) (Luke 18:31-34)

On the road to Jerusalem Jesus is reported to have predicted to the twelve apostles that he will be handed over to the Chief Priests, who will pass him to the Gentiles, who will mock him, spit on him, flog him and kill him, and after three days he will rise again.

[*Is this a case of the authors of the Gospels assuming that Jesus could foresee the future?*]

1.135: A Mother's Request (Matthew 20:20-28) (Mark 10:35-45)

The mother of Zebedee wants Jesus to confirm that her sons will sit on the right-hand side of Jesus in the kingdom of heaven.

Jesus' replies that this decision is God's and not his to grant (which says much about Jesus' idea about his Father being superior to him). It is not clear whether they are talking about the kingdom of heaven as imagined on earth, or above earth, in heaven.

When the others heard this, they started to argue. Jesus explained that in heaven, rulers do not lord it above everyone, as is the case on earth. Disciples must learn to be servants, first, if they expect to become great. The last will be first and the first will be last.

[*See also above Parable of the Labourers in the Vinyard.*]

1.136: The Healing of Two Blind men (Matthew 20:29-34) (Mark 10:46-52) (Luke 18:35-430

Here, two blind beggars, have faith in Jesus, who heals them.

1.137: Zacchaeus the Tax Collector (Luke 19:1-10)

Zacchaeus, a sinner, climbs a tree and is seen by Jesus. and is told by Jesus that he intends to stay in his house.

Zacchaeus declares that he will give up half his possessions and compensate generously those he has defrauded. Jesus forgives him his sins.

1.138: The Parable of the Pounds (Matthew 25:14-30) (Luke 19:11-27)

Scholars disagree about the exact meaning of these two stories and suggest that the stories may have been mixed up.

The conclusion that more will be given to all that have, and that from those who have nothing, more will be taken away, seems more like the judgment of a tyrant than of a fair-minded ruler.

[*Perhaps the wisest policy is to declare the meaning of this parable as 'obscure'.*]

THE DAYS IN JERUSALEM

1.139: Entry into Jerusalem (Matthew 21:1-8) (Mark 11:1-10) (Luke 19:28-38)

Jesus tells two disciples to go ahead and find a donkey and a colt tied with her, and to untie them and bring them to him.

This is reported to fulfil a prophecy in the Old Testament.

[*To me, it speaks of contacts with Jesus that the disciples knew nothing about. These are contacts with his promoters, who were watching and waiting to see what happened next, or they were already encouraging crowds to gather and welcome the entry of Jesus into Jerusalem, waving palm fronds, crying, 'Hosanna to the Son of David.'*]

1.140: Prediction of the Destruction of Jerusalem (Luke 18:39-44)

Luke says that Jesus predicted the rejection of him by the people of Jerusalem and the eventual destruction of the Temple by the Romans.

[*Does this more likely tell us when the Gospel of Luke was written. The authors knew when Jerusalem and the Temple were destroyed – it happened in AD 70.*]

1.141: Jesus Cleanses the Temple (Matthew 21:10-17) (Mark 11:11-19) (Luke 19:45-48)

Jesus went into the Temple and cleared out all who were selling and buying. He overturned the tables of money changers and the seats of those who sold doves for sacrifice. He said that God's house should be a house of prayer. *[This was a highly provocative act, designed to upset the Chief Priests and the scribes. It is surprising that Jesus wasn't arrested at this point and was allowed to leave the Temple.]* Luke suggests that he visited the Temple over several days and taught there, protected by crowds, who were spellbound at his teaching.

1.142: The Question about Jesus' Authority (Matthew 21:23-27) (Mark 11:27-33) (Luke 20:1-8)

A strange dialogue takes place with the chief priests, the scribes, and the elders in the temple, about the origins of John the Baptist. Jesus refuses to explain to them on what authority he himself was teaching in the Temple.

[It is not surprising if many people were confused about who Jesus was and about his mission. He was rarely forthcoming on the subject.]

1.143: The Parable of the Two Sons (Matthew 21:28-32)

This is a story about two sons. One son is told by his father to go into the vineyard. He refuses, but later he goes to the vineyard. The second son says he will go, but he doesn't. Jesus asks which son did the will of his father. The disciples say that the first son did the will of his father.

It is not clear if Jesus agrees with this answer. He responds bitterly by saying that the tax collectors and prostitutes will go to the kingdom of heaven ahead of them all. He adds that John had pointed the way of righteousness and had not been believed by many, but the tax collectors and prostitutes had believed him.

[This may reflect Jesus' view that salvation will be earned by the most unlikely people and not always by those who thought they were worthy. Does this have implications for all Christians?]

1.144: The Parable of the Tenants in the Vinyard
(Matthew 21:33-46) (Mark 12:1-12) (Luke 20:9-19)

The 'wicked' tenants in the parable are the Chief Priests and all who have authority in the Temple, who have rejected Jesus, who was sent by God.

[*This is either an example of an increasingly bitter Jesus, fully aware of the risks he is running in Jerusalem, or a literary device employed by the Gospel writers to highlight the status of Jesus as the Son of Man.*]

1.145: The Parable of the Wedding Banquet
(Matthew 22:1-14) (Luke14:16-24)

This is a further story that develops the theme of the rejection of Jesus, who had been sent by God to save the Jewish people.

Exasperated, a king tells his followers to go out and invite strangers to come and enjoy the prepared banquet.

[*This is another example where the Gospel writers are examining Jesus' story and justifying why most early Christians in the later first century were non-Jews. Their argument is that the Jews had rejected Jesus. Of course, Jews did not generally reject Jesus. Most of them were unaware of who Jesus might be. The Jewish authorities handed over Jesus to the Roman governor. And later, Jewish Christianity was largely wiped out in AD 70, when the Romans destroyed Jerusalem and its Temple.*]

1.146: Paying Taxes to Caesar (Matthew 22:15-22)
(Mark 12:20-26)

Jesus' enemies tried to trap him by asking him if they should pay taxes to the Roman Emperor. If Jesus said no, he would be guilty of opposing Rome; if he said yes, most Jews would have rejected Jesus.

Jesus was clever. He asked whose head was on the Roman coins used to pay tax. He said they should give to Caesar the things that were Caesar's and to God the things that were God's.

All parties were satisfied.

[But what if, in Jesus' mind, everything ultimately belonged to God?]

1.147: About the Resurrection (Matthew 22:22-33) (Mark 12:18-27) (Luke 20:27-40)

The Sadducees mentioned to Jesus that they did not believe in resurrection from the dead, and they asked him a difficult question about how he saw the status of a widow who has remarried. They asked: whose wife will she be in heaven?

Jesus explained that in heaven there is no marriage. The widow will be like an angel and be a child of God. Jesus' answer astounded his hearers.

[It would be interesting to ask members of any church congregation in 2022, 'How do you imagine life in heaven?']

1.148: The Great Commandment (Matthew 22:34-40) (Mark 12:28-34) (Luke 10:25-28)

Jesus was asked which is the greatest commandment. He answered, 'You shall love the Lord your God with all your heart, and with all your mind, and with all your strength. A second is this, you shall love your neighbour as yourself.'

Critically, Jesus acknowledges that 'this is much more important than whole burnt offerings and sacrifices.'

[This last comment needs noting. Surely, the comment can be interpreted to also refer to any excess praise or ritual in a modern church?]

1.149: About David's Son (Matthew 22:41-36) (Mark 12:35-37a) (Luke 20:41-44)

The 'Son of David' was a traditional title for the Messiah. David was seen as the author of Psalm 110, where this title is used. However, many modern scholars question David's authorship of the Psalms.

It is believed that, here, Jesus was implying that his status was more than a Son of David. (See *New Bible Commentary*, 1994, p934)

1.150: Jesus Denounces Scribes and Pharisees (Matthew 23:1-36) (Mark 12:37b-40) (Luke 20:45-47)

Here, we have a long section that suggests that the scribes and Pharisees did not practice what they preach.

[*This passage contains nothing of the selfless love and theme of forgiveness that one normally associates with Jesus' teaching. Can one conclude that this reflects the Gospel writers' idea of what Jesus should have said? Either that or this passage describes a very human Jesus: a Jesus suffering from disappointment, and angry at the prospect of being rejected, and very down in spirit?*]

1.151: Lament over Jerusalem (Matthew 23:37-39) (Luke 13: 34-35)

This is more written in the spirit of the above passage. The Gospel writers were expecting that Jesus would return soon and be hailed as one who 'comes in the name of the Lord.'

[*Note that this passage does not seem to imply that Jesus will have the status of God, but rather he would be the 'authorized representative of God'.*]

1.152: The Widow's Gift (Mark 12:41-44) (Luke 21:1-4):

The widow's contribution of a 'penny' to the Temple is all that she has got. Others have contributed a portion of their wealth. Hence her gift is a great value to her.

1.153: Jesus Speaks of the Destruction of the Temple: (Matthew 24:1-8) (Mark 13:1-8) Luke 21:5-11)

Jesus predicts the destruction of the Temple.

[*Is this demonstrating the beliefs of the Gospel writers who were writing after AD 70, that Jesus knew what would happen in the future?*]

The 'end of the Age' is referred to and is predicted to follow 'nation rising up against nation, kingdom against kingdom'. This may reflect the later beliefs that these things would occur and be heralded with famines, storms, and earthquakes – as 'signs' sent by God.

[*Do we, today, believe that God sends these disasters as warnings? Or that God causes famines, storms, or earthquakes?*]

1.154: The Coming Persecution (Matthew 24:9-14) (Mark 13:9-13) (Luke 21:12-19)

All the Gospel writers suggest that Jesus anticipated the persecution of his followers in the coming decades, and the fact that many disciples would fall away.

[*Were the Gospel writers putting their experiences into the mouth of the historical Jesus, to magnify him?*]

1.155: The Awful Horror (Matthew 24:15-28) (Mark 13:14-23) (Luke 21:20-26)

This is a woeful passage predicting what may happen at the end of the Age. This was thought to precede the Day of Judgement.

It speaks of 'suffering, such as has not been seen since the beginning of the world' and of a period of God's vengeance in accordance with what is written in ancient Hebrew Scripture.

[*They are presented as the words of Jesus, but one may wonder if they reflect the ideas of the authors of the Gospels, based on what they knew was going to be the fate of Jerusalem, well before the Gospels were written in their final form.*

It is also suggested by the Gospels writers that false Messiahs will arise that may even mislead the 'elect'. The 'elect' are the chosen ones of God, even if they are not aware of it.]

When Jesus returns (his *Parousia*), it is said that it will be as obvious as a flash of lightning. But the day and the hour are unknown except to God (Matthew 24:34-36) (Mark 13:30-32) (Luke 21:30-33).

1.156: The Need for Watchfulness (Mark 13:33-37) (Luke 21:34-46)

The message in this story is to keep awake and be prepared, at all times. (See also Matthew 24:24-51 and 25:1-30.)

1.157: The Last Judgement (Matthew 25:31-46)

This is when Jesus will return with all his angels. Like a shepherd, he will separate the sheep from the goats.

The sheep are those who will inherit the kingdom of heaven. We are told that they gave food to Jesus when he was hungry, he was a stranger and they received him in their homes, they clothed him when he was naked, cared for him when he was sick, and visited him in prison. Jesus later added that every time they helped those in need, it was as though they were helping him.

The goats did not do these things and will suffer eternal punishment.

[The key point here is that the criteria for eternal judgment have nothing to do with believing in Jesus or doing things in his name. Nor are they about praying or forms of worship in a church.

They are about a person adopting the mindset of Jesus and doing things because they believe in helping others and doing things without any expectation of reward, except the satisfaction of helping others.

Question: Where does this leave many Christians who emphasise the importance of charismatic worship of Jesus as God, or as God and a king?]

1.158: Days in Jerusalem (Luke 21:36-37)

Jesus taught in the Temple 'every' day and spent the night on the Mount of Olives. People came each day to listen to him speak.

[Jesus taught in the Temple, but he went to the Mount of Olives to pray – a quiet place.]

THE PASSION NARRATIVE

1.159: The Conspiracy Against Jesus (Matthew 26:1-5) (Mark 14:1-2) (Luke 22:1-2)

After saying various things, Jesus is alleged to have told his disciples that the Passover was coming in two days, and the 'Son of Man' would be handed over to be crucified.

[*Is this a case where the Gospel authors were putting words into the mouth of Jesus from their knowledge of what happened?*]

The passage also indicates that the High Priest called Caiaphas, with other chief priests and elders, met in the palace of the High Priest and planned to kill Jesus after the Passover festival.

1.160: The Anointing at Bethany (Matthew 26:6-13) (Mark 14:3-9)

While Jesus was at Bethany, in the house of Simon the leper, a woman came with an alabaster jar containing expensive ointment, which she poured on Jesus' head.

The disciples were horrified, as the ointment was expensive.

Jesus saw this as an act of preparation for his death. He said that the act of this woman should be told in remembrance of him, wherever the 'good news' is proclaimed in the whole world.

[*It seems that the Church has chosen to ignore this request, except as an occasional reading from the Bible.*]

1.161: Judas Agrees to Betray Jesus (Matthew 26:14-16) (Mark 14: 10-11) (Luke 22:3-6)

All three Gospel writers tell the tale of Judas Iscariot going to the Temple authorities and agreeing to betray Jesus for a sum of money.

1.162: Preparation for the Passover (Matthew 26:17-19) (Mark 14:12-16) (Luke 22:7-13)

On the first day of Unleavened Bread, when the Passover Lamb was to be sacrificed, Jesus sent Peter and John into Jerusalem with instructions to follow a man carrying a jar of water. They were to identify the house he went to and ask to see the guest room where they could all eat the Passover meal.

[*This is another strange request that hints of Jesus' contacts in Jerusalem: contacts that the disciples were unaware of. It suggests that there are many additional things that we are not told about in the Gospel stories.*]

THE LAST SUPPER

1.163: The Traitor (Matthew 26:20-25) (Mark 14:17-21) (Luke 22:14, 21-23)

Jesus announces that he will be betrayed. Judas is present.

As with many other aspects of Jesus' story, the betrayal is described as happening because 'it is written'. Judas was acting out a part already prophesied.

[*Was Judas carrying out Jesus' secret instructions?*]

1.164: The Last Supper (Matthew 26:26-29) (Mark 14:22-25) (Luke 22:15-23)

Jesus asked them to remember him when they dine in the future. He said that they should break the bread and eat it in remembrance of his life and death, given for them. Similarly, they should take the cup and drink wine, remembering that he shed his blood for them.

This was a simple, moving act, that the early Church later turned into a formal ritual and eventually made into a sacrament.

[*It could have been remembered as a simple act, to be performed at special times by all followers of Jesus, privately, in their homes at a family celebration. Or, it could have been celebrated in both ways: one when Jesus' followers met formally together in fellowship and secondly, informally, when the occasion was remembered as a family celebration.*]

[*Was this a lost opportunity to embed the remembrance of Jesus, in the Christian home and away from a church?*]

1.165: Greatness in the kingdom of God
(Luke 22:24-30)

An interesting dispute is recorded about who among them would be greatest in the future, but Jesus stressed that he is among them as a servant, and they must also see themselves in the same role.

[*This idea of their being no hierarchy in heaven is mentioned several times in the Gospel but it seems to have been ignored by the Church.*]

Jesus added that he conferred on them a kingdom: they would sit on thrones, judging the twelve tribes of Israel.

[*If these are to be believed as the words of Jesus, it may confirm the view that Jesus never had ideas of promoting a church composed mainly of gentiles and that his remit was to the sinners among the Jews.*

Nevertheless, much of Jesus' teaching, potentially, has universal application. It aims to develop harmony among all communities and nations on earth.]

1.166: Peter's Denial (Luke 26: 30-35)
(Mark 14:26-31) (Luke:22-38):

First, Jesus tells them that they will all initially desert him, then he will go ahead and meet them again in Galilee. Peter denied this will happen, but Jesus told him that, that very night, he would betray him three times.

1.167: Jesus in Gethsemane (Matthew 26:36-46)
(Mark 14:32-42) (Like 22:40-46)

Jesus takes Peter and James and John to Gethsemane. He goes away from them to pray to his Father and asks God to remove his task from him.

Jesus returns and finds the disciples sleeping.

He goes to pray for second time and returns. Again, they are asleep.

After praying for a third time, he wakes them and tells them that the 'Son of Man' is betrayed, and that the betrayer is near.

1.168: Jesus is Taken Captive (Matthew 26:47-56) (Mark 14:43-52) (Luke 22:47-53)

Jesus is arrested, but in the process, one of his disciples resorts to violence and one of the high priest's men has his ear cut off. Great stress is placed on the fact that everything has occurred in accordance with ancient prophecies.

After his arrest, Jesus' disciples desert him.

1.169: Jesus before the Council (Matthew 26:57-75) (Mark 14:53-72) (Luke 22:54-71)

Peter follows and is seen by a girl. Three times, Peter denies knowing Jesus.

Jesus is mocked and beaten. He said enough for the high priest to declare Jesus' words as blasphemy, and it was agreed that he deserved to die. They handed Jesus over to Pontius Pilate for judgment.

1.170: The Death of Judas (Matthew 27:3-10)

Matthew reports that Judas hanged himself.

1.171: The Trial before Pilate (Matthew 27:11-14) (Mark 15:2-5) (Luke 23:2-5)

The Gospel writers say that Jesus made no answer to Pilate and Pilate could find no fault with Jesus.

[*A more likely explanation is that the Gospel writers hesitated to suggest that the Roman Governor found Jesus guilty, because early Christians needed to live and thrive in the Roman Empire. It was a known fact that the Romans crucified Jesus, but the Jewish authorities were blamed as being responsible for Jesus' death.*]

1.172: Jesus before Herod (Luke 23:6-16)

Herod Antipas was in Jerusalem. It is suggested that Pilate sent Jesus to Herod. However, it appears that Herod was wise enough to send Jesus back to Pilate, for him to decide what to do with him.

1.173: Sentence of Death (Matthew 27:15-26) (Mark 15:6-15) (Luke 23:17-25)

This is a confusing tale of Pilate asking a crowd to decide who should be pardoned – Jesus or a prisoner called Barabbas (This means 'Son of the Father'). The crowd chose Barabbas and Jesus was condemned to be crucified.

1.174: Mocking of Jesus by the Soldiers (Matthew 27:27-31) (Mark 15:16-20)

The soldiers mocked Jesus and put a robe on him and a crown of thorns, before leading him to be crucified.

1.175: The Crucifixion (Matthew 27:32-44) (Mark 15:22-32) (Luke 23:33-43)

It is reported that it was nine o'clock in the morning when they crucified Jesus, with two others.

Jesus is reported as saying, 'Father, forgive them for they know not what they do.'

[*This is significant. At the last moment, Jesus is emphasizing the importance of forgiveness, not condemnation.*]

At three o'clock, Jesus is reported as crying out, 'My God, my God, why have you forsaken me?' The Gospel writers interpreted this as a quotation from Isaiah.

[*This could also have been Jesus' genuine human reaction, when he realized that there had been no intervention by the people, or by angels, to save him.*]

As Jesus died, it was said that the curtain in the Temple was torn in two.

[*Is this a bit of artistic license?*]

Mary Magdalene, Mary the mother of James and Jose, and Salome, were said to have watched from a distance.

1.176: The Burial of Jesus (Matthew 27:57-66) (Mark 15:42-47) (Luke 23:50-56)

Joseph of Arimathea is reported to have obtained Pilate's permission to take the body of Jesus for burial in a tomb owned by Joseph.

Jesus' body was placed in the tomb and a stone was rolled over the entrance.

Mary Magdalene and Mary, the mother of Jose, watched from nearby.

Next day, a guard was placed at the tomb.

1.177: The Empty Tomb (Matthew 28:1-10) (Mark 16:1-8) (Luke 24:1-12)

On the morning after the Sabbath, Mary Magdalene and Mary the mother of Jose went to the tomb with spices, to anoint Jesus' body.

Matthew tells us that there was an earthquake, and an angel of the Lord descended from heaven and rolled back the stone covering the tomb's entrance. Mark and Luke say that the women found the stone rolled back.

In Matthew, the angel speaks to the terrified women and says that Jesus has risen from the dead and gone ahead into

Galilee, where they will see him. In Mark, this information is communicated by a young man in a white robe. In Luke, it is two men in dazzling clothes who say the same thing. In Matthew, the women see Jesus who speaks to them.

In Luke, Mary Magdalene, Mary the mother of James, Joanna and other women, explained to the apostles about Jesus rising from the dead. Peter went to the tomb, only to find it empty apart from some linen cloths.

Later (Matthew 28:11-15) it is suggested that the chief priests gave money to the tomb guard to say that the disciples removed Jesus' body by night and that this is what Jews are taught 'to this day'.

1.178: The Commissioning of the Disciples (Matthew 28:16-2000)

Matthew writes that the eleven disciples went to Galilee and saw Jesus – but some doubted. It is added that Jesus said that 'all authority in heaven and earth' had been given to him and that they should now go and 'make disciples of all nations' and that he would be with them to 'the end of the age'.

[*Is this a case of the Gospel writers imagining what they believed Jesus might have said?*]

1.179: Road to Emmaus (Luke 24:13-53)

Luke says that two disciples went to Emmaus, some seven miles from Jerusalem and were met on their way by Jesus (although they did not recognize him). He explained about how necessary the crucifixion and resurrection had been: both had been prophesied. They recognized the man as Jesus when they dined and he took bread, blessed it, and broke it. He vanished from their sight at that point.

Luke writes that Jesus appeared to the disciples again, and they had opportunities to hear him speak and see his wounds. Their task now was to 'witness all these things' and proclaim

repentance and forgiveness of sins in his name to all nations.'
He then led them as far as Bethany, where he blessed them,
before he was carried up into heaven. After, they returned to
Jerusalem with great joy.

[*That Jesus was reported to have been carried up into the
heavens, reflects the traditional idea of heaven being above the
stars: a place from which angels could descend of wings. How
do modern Christians visualize heaven, today?*]

1.180: The Longer Ending of Mark (Mark 16:9-20)

Mark summarizes the events in a singe paragraph, saying that
after Jesus rose from the dead on the third day, he appeared to
Mary Magdalene. She told the disciples, but they would not
believe her. Later Jesus met two disciples who were walking in
the country, but their story was not believed by the others.
Later Jesus appeared to all the disciples

Jesus told them to go and proclaim the good news to 'the
whole creation'. He added that the one who believes and is
baptized will be saved – others will be condemned. Believers
will 'cast out demons, speak in new tongues, pick up snakes
and eat deadly things but will not be harmed, and they will lay
their hands on the sick and they will recover'.

[*Are these reflecting how the Gospel writers interpreted the
words of Jesus, spoken many years previously?*]

Later Mark adds that Jesus was taken up into heaven
where he 'sits at the right-hand side of God.'

[*Whichever way you interpret this image of Jesus, it does
not seem to add up to full equality with God?*]

END OF NOTES ON THE SYNOPTIC GOSPELS

PART TWO

THE GOSPEL OF JOHN

NOTES BY HARRY HOULDSWORTH

2.1: Treatment of this Gospel

I have not identified many key passages in John. This is because it would involve the unnecessary repetition of the points that have been made above, when considering the content of the Synoptic Gospels of Matthew, Mark and Luke.

The Gospel of John was written later than the Synoptic Gospels, possibly at the end of the first century and the tone of the Gospel of John is identified in the first chapter.

2.2: Chapter 1:

John the Baptist denies being the Christ.

Verses 19 to 23: John the Baptist denies being the Christ, or being Elijah, or being the Prophet. He says, 'I am the voice of one calling in the desert, "Make straight the way for the Lord".'

Verses 29 -34: John sees Jesus coming towards him and he says: 'Look, the Lamb of God, who takes away the sin of the world!'

<u>Thus, in the Gospel of John, Jesus is proclaimed immediately as the living Word, the Christ, and sacrificial 'lamb of God', whose mission is to die and take away the sins of the world.</u>

[*This is unlike in the above Synoptic Gospels, where who Jesus is, is not revealed fully, and Jesus often tells his disciples to keep his activities secret.*]

In this last Gospel, John the Baptist says of Jesus: 'I myself did not know him, but the reason I came baptizing with water was that he might be revealed to Israel.'

[*There is no indication here that Jesus and John might be related and that their mothers knew one another, and that John and Jesus might have had an understanding about each other's status.*]

John adds: 'The man on whom you see the Spirit come down and remain is he who will baptize with the Holy Spirit. I have seen and I testify that this is the Son of God.'

[*This quickly established that the key message of the Gospel of John is that Jesus is the 'Son of God, the Christ'.*]

Contrast this approach with that in the other Gospels, where a much more down-to-earth image of Jesus is presented.

[*In Matthew, Mark and Luke, Jesus is portrayed as a teacher and a healer, and someone who might be the expected Messiah. Jesus often calls himself the Son of Man. This is a portrait of the Jesus that was seen by most people while he was alive.*

Most of Jesus' contemporaries would have been horrified to have been told that Jesus was in some way divine.]

2.3: Chapters 2-21:

The Gospel of John demonstrates how much the idea of who Jesus was had been firmed up in the sixty years or so since his death – that is, before the Gospel of John was either written or finished, and throughout the Gospel of John, the author writes confidently about Jesus as the Christ, the Son of God. There is less emphasis on the poor, or on Jesus' use of parables.

The Gospel is beautifully written in poetic language. It is a pleasure to read and consider, in the light of the many questions and comments that have been raised in the above notes on the Synoptic Gospels.

2.4: Chapter 6-22-30 (The Unbelief of the Jews)

Critically, the Gospel of John was written after Jewish Christianity in Palestine was largely destroyed in AD 70.

This was in a period when new Christian communities were emerging in towns in Greece and Asia Minor, alongside longer-established Jewish communities with whom the Christians were increasingly at loggerheads.

Chapter Six speaks of the unbelief of the 'Jews' in a way that is unhelpful. The Jews are being blamed for Jesus' death and this would eventually produce strong anti-Jewish feelings in Europe.

END OF NOTES ON THE GOSPEL OF JOHN

PART THREE

ACTS OF THE APOSTLES

NOTES BY HARRY HOULDSWORTH

3.01: Summary of *Acts of the Apostles*

This is the fascinating story of the acts of Paul and other apostles, as Christianity was preached outside of Palestine. It starts in Palestine with Jesus being taken up into heaven and Matthias being chosen to replace Judas Iscariot. The coming of the Holy Spirit at Pentecost is described, as is the life of early Christians awaiting the return of Jesus. The death of Stephen is reported. Saul of Tarsus is introduced, and details are given of his conversion. The missionary journeys of Paul are covered, as is his later arrest in Jerusalem and his voyage as a prisoner to Rome.

The *Notes* cover key chapters only.

3.02: Chapter 1

Acts reports that the disciples met with the risen Jesus several times over a period of forty days after the Resurrection, before Jesus was 'taken up before their very eyes, and a cloud hid him from their sight.'

While they were looking up into the sky, two men 'dressed in white' asked them why they were standing there 'looking into the sky. They were told that 'Jesus has been taken . . . into heaven,' and he 'will come back in the same way you have seen him go to heaven.'

[This confirms the traditional understanding of a three-tiered universe: with heaven above the clouds, from which angels with wings could descend. The disciples and Paul firmly

believed that Jesus would return this way in a very short time.
This did not happen, and it begs the question: 'Do we, in the
twenty-first century, need to revise our ideas about the
reliability of some biblical ideas?']

In Chapter 1 of *Acts*, the first 'believers of the Way ' are
described as numbering about 'a hundred and twenty.' The
eleven disciples choose Matthias, by lots, to replace Judas.

3.03: Chapter 2

The Holy Spirit at Pentecost (Acts 2: 1-13):

This critical event is described: 'Suddenly a sound like the
blowing of a violent wind came from heaven and filled the
whole house where they were sitting. They saw what seemed
to be tongues of fire that separated and came to rest on each of
them. All of them were filled with the Holy Spirit and began to
speak in other tongues as the spirit enabled them.'

[*This passage has traditionally been interpreted literally and
the apostles are said to have been able to speak in many languages.*

*More recent commentators have focused on the poetic
language used in the passage, suggesting that 'like a blowing
wind' and 'what seemed like tongues of fire,' should be
interpreted poetically, not literally, and that the presence of the
Holy Spirit produced 'burning enthusiasm' and ecstatic
utterances that communicated their enthusiasm as 'glossolalia'
– sounds that anyone could appreciate regardless of their
native language. The fact that some thought that the apostles
had 'had too much wine,' may confirm this more natural
interpretation. (See H A Guy, Acts of the Apostles, c1952)*

Vs 17-23: Peter quotes from Joel to explain how the Holy
Spirit will come in 'the last days.' This endorses the apostles'
views that the 'last days' were already here and that Jesus' life
was clearly endorsed by prophesies in Hebrew Scripture.

V38: Peter calls on the hearers, outside in the town, to
'Repent and be baptized . . . in the name of Jesus Christ for the

forgiveness of your sins. And you will receive the gift of the Holy Spirit.' We are told that about 3000 accepted Peter's call.

V39: Believers devoted themselves to the teaching of the apostles, to the breaking of bread and to prayer. They practiced Christian communism: selling possessions and goods, giving to the needy, and praising God. *(Christian communism was not practiced for many years. It appears to have died out when Jesus did not quickly return to earth.)*]

3.04: Chapter 3

V6: Peter cures a crippled person.

[*Many may wonder why priests are unable to do the same sort of thing in the twenty-first century. If miracles happened 2000 years, ago, why not in 2022?*]

V19: More calls from Peter to 'Repent!'

V21: Peter explains that Jesus must remain in heaven until God decides to restore everything that the prophets prophesied. [*Note that there is a clear distinction here between God and Jesus.*]

3.05: Chapter 4

Peter and John are brought before the Sanhedrin in Jerusalem for proclaiming the resurrection of the dead and healing the cripple. Eventually, they were released. The coming of the Holy Spirit was linked to an earthquake that shook buildings.

V3: Peter accuses Annanias of keeping back some money he had received when selling his land, whereupon poor Annanias fell down dead. He wife suffered the same fate for failing to tell the truth. [*Would a loving God cause such things to happen? If he does, why does this not happen today?*]

V17: More healings and miracles follow as crowds bring their sick to be healed. [*Why not today, also as part of missionary activities?*]

V18: The apostles were later arrested, but during the night an angel of the Lord opened the prison doors and let them out. [*Why does this sort of thing happen today?*]

V34: Gamalial, a respected Pharisee, advised caution to the Sanhedrin and the apostles were released, after being flogged. They continued to preach.

3.06: Chapter 6

As more were converted, new leaders were required, and Stephen was among them. He quickly gained a reputation for doing 'great wonders' and 'miraculous signs' among the people.

3.07: Chapter 7

Stephen was brought before the Sanhedrin and he gave them a long lecture on Hebrew history, causing the Jewish leaders to 'gnash their teeth.' When Stephen said, 'I see the heaven open and the Son of man standing at the right-hand side of God,' they were appalled.

[*Note that the Son of Man and God are here seen as separate entities.*]

Stephen was taken outside and stoned to death. We are told that 'Saul' witnessed and approved of Stephen's death.

3.08: Chapter 8

A great persecution of Christians followed, with Saul taking a leading role. He 'dragged off men and women to prison.'

The career of Philip is described in Samaria, as he cast-out many evil spirits from sick persons.

Vs 28-40 cover the story of Philip and the Ethiopian eunuch. Philip baptizes him and demonstrates how gentiles are welcome as 'Christians'.

3.09: Chapter 9

This is the story of Saul's conversion and his later acceptance by the apostles in Jerusalem.

Later, (as Paul), Paul said that Jesus spoke to him directly when he suffered sunstroke or had a mental breakdown and that it was through Jesus that he learned what to believe. This included his belief that Jesus was resurrected from the dead and Paul said that without this belief, his Christianity was nothing.

Paul later repeated his claim that he received his faith directly from Jesus, in dreams, but this conflicts with the evidence that, prior to his conversion, Saul spent a long period arresting and interrogating Christians, who must have told him a similar story – which Saul refused to accept, until after his mental breakdown.

This explains the probable main source of Paul's knowledge about Christian beliefs. Later, he may have imagined that Jesus was speaking directly to him in dreams. Note that this must make Paul one of the earliest 'Gnostics'. (The Gnostics were later condemned by the Church for believing that the Holy Spirit could guide believers in individual ways.) [*The point is that Saul's conversion is easily explained. He learned about Christianity from the many Christians he interrogated.*]

Vs 38-42: Peter raises a woman (Tabitha) from the dead. [*If it could be done then, why not today?*]

3.10: Chapters 10 and 11

Cornelius is described as God-fearing. He is a Roman soldier and the first important gentile to be baptized.

V11: Peter had a vision of a large sheet being let down from heaven, holding animals and birds, that God said he was to eat. He interpreted this dream as telling him that the Jewish food-laws were restrictive and did not need to apply to Christians.

When he was invited into Cornelius' house, he gladly accepted the invitation, even though Cornelius was a gentile. Later, Peter explained his change of heart to others.

In this lengthy story, the Holy Spirit was received by gentiles as well as by Jews. It was a new chapter in Christianity – the mission of the apostles to all nations, and it followed the persecution of Christians, after the stoning of Stephen.

Vs 25-26: Barnabas travelled to Tarsus to look for Saul and brought him to Antioch, where for a year Paul met and studied with Christians. [*We are informed that it was in Antioch that the disciples were first called 'Christians'.*]

Vs 27-30: Agabus came from Jerusalem to Antioch and prophesied a coming famine in the entire Roman world. This is said to have happened in the reign of the Claudius (AD 41-54). This suggests a date of about AD 40 for events at Antioch.

The Christian community in Antioch provided for their brothers in Judea and sent the aid to the elders by Barnabas and Saul. [*This is early evidence of Christianity in practice, seeking to alleviate suffering in the world.*]

3.11: Chapter 12

At this time, King 'Herod' (Herod Agrippa 11, born AD 10.) had 'James the brother of John' killed 'by the sword' (some 11 years after the death of Stephen). Herod also had Peter arrested and closely guarded.

We are informed that an angel appeared to Peter and his chains 'fell off' and he walked out past the guards, and that the prison doors opened for them.' It is said that Herod executed the prison guards, and that Herod was later killed by an 'angel of the Lord'. [*Again, if this happened like this, then, why can it not happen like this in 2022?*]

3.12: Chapter 13

This chapter tells of the first Missionary Journey by Saul and Barnabas. From this point Saul is referred to as 'Paul'. Paul is filled with the Holy Spirit and causes a Elymas, the sorcerer, to go blind, thus impressing the proconsul in Paphos. [*Did the man go blind naturally, and did Christians then believe that Paul had caused this? We can never know the truth.*]

(V38) In Pisidian Antioch Paul taught his key message in synagogues that 'through Jesus, the forgiveness of sins is proclaimed' and that 'everyone who believes is justified from everything that could not be justified from by the law of Moses.'

Paul explained to orthodox Jews that, because they had rejected his message, he was now turning to the Gentiles, in accordance with God's wishes. Many Gentiles were converted and, sadly, friction with orthodox Jews became a constant problem for Paul and the new Church.

3.13: Chapter 14

At Iconium, this division occurred again between Jews and Gentile Christians and Barnabas and Paul had to flee to Lystra and Derbe, to preach in safety.

At Lystra, Paul healed a cripple. But later, the Jewish communities became hostile to Paul's teaching and he and Barnabas had to move on.

3.14: Chapter 15

When they returned to Jerusalem, Paul and Barnabas attended a Council meeting, which discussed again the issue of Gentiles becoming Christians, and what Jewish laws they needed to observe.

A compromise seems to have been reached. Gentiles were required only to abstain from food sacrificed to idols, from blood, from meat of strangled animals, and from sexual immorality.

3.15: Chapter 16

Timothy joined Paul and Silas. Note that Paul 'circumcised Timothy because of the Jews who lived where they were going.'

V14: Paul baptized Lydia and her household in Philippi. She was a successful businesswoman and a 'seller of purple cloth'. Paul stayed with her, and Lydia became an important supporter of Paul.

V19: The owners of a slave girl were responsible for having Paul and Silas imprisoned, because Paul had reduced her value by exorcising the 'spirit within her' that enabled her to tell fortunes. Note that this event is followed by another miraculous escape from prison.

3.16: Chapter 17

Paul arrived in Thessalonica and successfully persuaded Greeks that Scripture explained why Jesus had to suffer and rise from the dead. There was more friction with members of the local Jewish community, so they moved on and were more successful in the next town of Berea.

Vs 16-32: Paul preached in Athens to Epicurean and Stoic philosophers. Paul spoke to a meeting of the Areopagus and referred to their altar to an 'UNKNOWN GOD'. Paul told them about the Hebrew God and the call for all to repent before final judgment.

Some Athenians were skeptical about the idea of the resurrection of the dead. But we are told that many were interested, including a woman named Damaris.

[*Note that Paul used a successful teaching technique, by finding something they could all agree on to interest the intelligent Athenians – THE UNKNOWN GOD. (There is a lesson here for mission in the twenty-first century – always find some shared beliefs.)*]

3.17: Chapter 18

In Corinth, we learn of another woman: Priscilla, the wife of Aquila. We learn also that Paul was a tentmaker 'as they were'. Paul stayed in Corinth for 'a year and a half.'

3.18: Chapter 19

Paul moved to Ephesus and met people who had received 'John's baptism.' Paul explained that 'John's baptism was a baptism of repentance' and that John taught of the coming of Jesus. The Ephesians were baptized again by Paul, who laid hands on them, and they received the Holy Spirit, and they 'spoke in tongues and prophesied.' He preached in Ephesus and in the synagogue for three months.

V11: 'God did extraordinary miracles through Paul, so that even handkerchiefs and aprons that had touched him were taken to the sick, and their illnesses were cured, and the evil spirits left them.' *(This thinking was taken up by many Christians in the later centuries.)*

V15: This includes further tales of the casting out of evil spirits and how this impressed local people.

3.19: Chapter 20

Paul travelled to Macedonia and Greece. At Troas, Paul is reported as raising a young man called Eutychus from the dead, after Eutychus fell from a high window. [*The writer of Acts believes that Paul achieved this. Do we, today?*]

3.20: Chapter 21

Paul returned to Jerusalem, where disagreements about Gentiles being baptized re-surfaced. Paul was arrested. He defended himself and claimed to be a Roman citizen.

3.21: Chapter 23

V 8: Before the Sanhedrin, the divisions between Pharisees and Sadducees were made clear. Paul stated that he was a Pharisee and like them had hope in the resurrection of the dead. The Sadducees, by contrast, said 'that there is no resurrection, and that there are neither angels nor spirits.'

V12. There was a plot to kill Paul. Paul was transferred to Caesarea, where he was brought before Felix, the governor.

V14: Paul said: 'I admit that I worship the God of our fathers as a follower of the Way, which they call a sect. I believe everything that agrees with the Law and that is written by the Prophets, and I have the same hope in God as these men, that there will be a resurrection of both the righteous and the wicked.' He added that 'It is concerning the resurrection of the dead that I am on trial before you today.' (V 21)

V 27: Two years passed, before Felix died. Paul was still in prison. Festus became governor of the province.

3.22: Chapter 25

The trial before Festus. Finally, King Agrippa and Festus found Paul innocent but as Paul had appealed to Rome, he was sent to Rome as a prisoner, to be tried by Caesar.

3.23: Chapter 27

Paul sailed for Rome. Fourteen days after leaving Crete, their ship was shipwrecked on Malta where the survivors were kindly received. Paul laid his hands on the son of the governor and healed him.

3.24: Chapter 28

Eventually, they reached Puteoli, in Italy, where they found some 'brothers' who invited them to spend a week with them.

When they arrived in Rome, Paul was allowed to live by himself with a soldier to guard him. In Rome, Paul preached to the Jews.

V30,31, Acts, ends with the words: 'For two whole years Paul stayed there in his own rented house and welcomed all who came to see him. Boldly and without hindrance he preached the kingdom of God and taught about the Lord Jesus Christ.'

END OF NOTES ON ACTS

*

PART FOUR

LETTERS FROM PAUL AND OTHERS

NOTES BY HARRY HOULDSWORTH

Note that the Letters predate the main Gospels.
The key points only are summarized.

4.01: *ROMANS*

4.01.01: God's Wrath Against Mankind (Romans 1:18-32)

God's wrath is plainly revealed from the heavens against all godlessness and wickedness.

Paul believed that God's eternal power and divine nature have been clearly seen by 'men' since the creation of the world.

He writes that men have worshipped false images of God that look like birds, animals, and reptiles. They have exhibited sexual impurities and degraded their bodies. They have not praised God as the true Creator.

Even women changed natural relations for unnatural relations, as did men, who committed indecent acts with other men. *(Note that it is only recently that western governments have adopted a tolerant approach to homosexuality.)*

Paul wrote that men and women have become filled with every kind of wickedness, evil, greed, and depravity. They are full of envy, murder, strife, deceit, and malice. They are gossips, slanderers, God-haters, insolent, arrogant, boastful. They invent ways of doing evil, they disobey their parents, and are heartless, senseless, and ruthless.

Paul wrote that: 'People who do these things deserve death.' A more reasonable conclusion might have been to affirm that true Christians do not 'do these things'.

4.1.02: God's Righteous Judgment (2:1-16)

Paul writes: Do not be hypocrites and pass judgment on others for doing the above things, while you continue to commit these sins yourself. You will be judged and punished according to your sins. *(This confirms that a Christian life is about 'doing'- applying faith, day in day out.)*

4.01.03: Justification by Faith (Ch 3 and 4)

This is a major theme of St Paul. We are all justified by faith, not by our good works.

<u>Martin Luther built the Reformation on this theme.</u>

Martin Luther had a big political agenda that included challenging the practices and authority of the Roman Catholic Church, but 'Justification by Faith' can be over-simplified and become, simply a requirement to believe that Jesus is the Son of God, with a view that good works are of less importance: thus – 'believing' becomes more important than 'doing'.

Jesus' parable of the Good Samaritan and the Parable of the Sheep and Goats (about Final judgment) stand as stark challenges to Luther, but not of St Paul. The Good Samaritan and those who were saved, were saved because they instinctively believed in the same Gospel of unselfish love that was taught by Jesus and they practiced it without any expectation of reward – this was a measure of their belief (their faith in the importance of unselfish love in their lives). In this sense 'faith' is more directly linked to Jesus' teaching than to one's comprehension of who Jesus is or was.

[Surely, this is not difficult to understand. <u>What Jesus taught and who he was are two separate subjects.</u> What he taught is relatively easy to understand, if difficult to put into practice. Who Jesus was is a complex academic debate which continues to inflame opposing opinions. What is meant by 'divinity' is beyond the experience of even the best human brain and can only be understood via poetic language, using metaphors. A loving God will understand this.]

96

[The idea that God is very angry with humanity comes out of the Old Testament and St Paul enthusiastically supported this view, even though the very idea conflicts with Jesus' teaching about love and forgiveness.]

4.01.04: We are Living Sacrifices (Ch 12)

People have different gifts (such as prophesying, serving, teaching, encouraging, contributing to the needs of others, leadership, being merciful).

The importance of UNSELFISH LOVE is highlighted:

Love must be sincere. Cling to what is good. Be devoted to others who believe in unselfish love. Honour one another. Be joyful in serving the Lord, and in prayer. Be patient in affliction. Practice hospitality. Bless those who persecute you. Do not curse. Live in harmony with others. Be humble and willing to associate with all levels in society. Do not be conceited. Do not repay evil with evil. Do what is right in the eyes of everybody. If possible, live at peace with everybody. Do not take revenge but let God judge. If your enemy is hungry feed him or her (you will change their hateful attitudes).

[You can do all these things and still have major debates about who Jesus was.]

4.01.05: Submission to Authorities (Ch 13)

Paul stressed that being a good citizen is second nature to a Christian.

Everyone must submit to governing authorities; pay taxes; give everyone what you owe them, honour others, love one another. Do not murder, steal, commit adultery, do not covet. Behave decently. Put aside the deeds of darkness and put on the armour of light. Make every effort to do what leads to peace. Please your neighbour wherever possible. Become a servant, as Jesus did.

[Paul here is being realistic. We all need to live with existing authorities. Otherwise, we may face penalties, fines, imprisonment.

In Paul's day, authorities were often harsh and unjust. Paul knew that Christians could not change things overnight. It was necessary for Christianity to survive in a hostile, unjust world.

Therefore, Christians should aim to be model citizens, acknowledging civil authorities, while also acknowledging God's overall authority. This explains why Paul urges women to obey their husband and slaves to obey those who own them. This was the real world in which early Christians lived.]

END OF NOTES ON ROMANS

4.2: 1 CORINTHIANS

4.02.01: Chapter 1

V10: Reference to divisions in the Christian Church in Corinth.

4.02.02: Chapter 2

V 11-15: 'For who among men knows the thoughts of a man, except the man's spirit within him? In the same way, no-one knows the thoughts of God except the Spirit of God. We have not received the spirit of the world but the Spirit who is from God, that we may understand what God has freely given to us.' Paul ends: 'But we have the mind of Christ.' *[Is having the mind of Christ more important than knowing who he is or was?]*

As apostles of Christ, those who have received the Spirit of God must remain faithful. Paul suggests that they should be cautious about judging people before 'the appointed time' when 'the Lord comes.'

This is an indication that Paul expected Jesus to return soon.

[The assumption by Paul seems to be that those who receive guidance by the Holy Spirit will all interpret it in the way God wishes them to. The Gnostics were later criticized for encouraging people to rely on their individual interpretations of what the Holy Spirit was telling them. This is the problem with spirit-led teaching: different people interpreted what the Holy Spirit was saying to them in highly

individual ways: who could know who was saying the right thing?]

4.02.03: Chapter 5

V 1: Paul refers to reports of sexual immorality among the Corinthian Christians. He returns to this theme later in the letter.

4.02.04: Chapter 6

V 1-11: Paul advises Christians against going to law, where they have a dispute among them, especially where the lawyers are non-Christian.

He reminds them of wicked acts: sexual immorality; idolatry; adultery; male prostitution; homosexuality; greed, drunkenness; slandering; swindling others. *He says that you cannot do these things and be sanctified and justified in the name of the Lord Jesus Christ and by the Spirit of the Lord. In other words, how you live is the litmus test of the state of your 'faith'. Faith alone is insufficient.*

4.02.05: Chapter 7 (Marriage)

To avoid immorality, each man should have his own wife and each woman her own husband. They both own one another's bodies. The implication is that too much sexual indulgence should be avoided.

Paul is not easy about sex, even in marriage. He advises widows and widowers to remain single, but 'if they cannot control themselves, they should marry, for it is better to marry than to burn with passion.'

Paul advises against divorce, even where the partner is not a Christian.

Note verses 21-24. Here Paul touches on slavery which was a fact of life for many people in Roman times. He suggests that a Christian slave must accept their situation, although if they can gain their freedom, they should do so.

Note verse 29, where Paul writes: 'What I mean brothers, is that time is short.' He adds: 'For this world in its present form is passing away.'

[As did Jesus, Paul thought that the kingdom of God was imminent, and, therefore, everyday concerns – such as looking for a wife, being concerned about material wealth, even being a slave – these things were not worth bothering about. Soon, these things would be irrelevant. This begs the question as to whether we in 2022 should have a different take on these issues, just in the same way that we now have a different take than Paul on homosexuality? We live in a different age.]

4.02.06: Ch 11:1-16 (Men and Women)

Paul writes: 'Now I want you to realise that the head of every man is Christ, and the head of the woman is man, and the head of Christ is God.' He explains that this is because a man is in the image of God, but the woman is the glory of man – as she came from Adam.

Paul says that a man who prays should have his head uncovered, but a woman should have her head covered.

[This illustrates that Paul had a literal understanding of the Creation Story in Genesis, which many people do not accept today, except as reflecting the social ideas of 2000 years ago – including the idea that a man should have short hair and a woman long hair as it is her 'glory'.]

4.02.07: Chapter 11 (The Lord's Supper)

Paul criticizes the Corinthian Christians for not showing sufficient respect when they have a common meal in memory of Jesus' 'Last Supper'.

Paul stresses that they should make a ritual of the meal and eat the bread and drink the wine in an orderly fashion, because they are proclaiming Jesus' death until he comes again.

The words in Corinthians (Chapter 11: 23-25) are those which the Roman Church later incorporated into the Eucharist service in churches.

We do not know whether Paul was the first apostle to develop the idea of the Eucharistic meal. It was something he endorsed to celebrate Jesus' death – *but it is important to be aware that he was not focusing on the gory details of the crucifixion. He was celebrating Jesus' resurrection from the dead, which to early Christians gave vivid evidence that death was not the end, and that eternal life was being offered to those who believed in this 'Good News'.*

[For the first 300 years of Christianity, the crucifixion was a difficult subject, as it reminded Romans that Jesus had been condemned as an enemy of Rome. What needed highlighting was the outcome: the Resurrection story.]

4.02.08: Chapter 12 (Spiritual Gifts)

These come in various forms and include gifts of wisdom, ability to encourage knowledge or faith, to heal, to have the gift of miraculous powers, the gift to prophecy, or speaking in tongues or the interpretation of tongues.

[These reflect the ideas of 2000 years ago. Do they all apply today?]

Ch 12: 27-28: Some people are apostles, some are teachers, some can work miracles, others have the gift of healing or the ability to help others, or are administrators, or speak in tongues. Collectively, they make up the body of Christ: each Christian is one part of that whole body.

4.02.09: Chapter 13 (Love)

This is the passage that is often quoted at marriage services and even at funerals. Verse 13 sums up the passage: 'And now these three remain: faith, hope and love. But the greatest of these is love.'

Paul here expresses the firm conviction that, however important 'faith' is to a Christian, it is secondary to unselfish love, which is a motivator for everything that a Christian (or even a good non-Christian) thinks, says and does. Without evidence of unselfish love in action, 'faith' (even a Christian faith) is rendered unsatisfactory. [Did Martin Luther get it wrong?]

4.02.10: Chapter 14 (Orderly Worship)

The main theme of this chapter is 'having constructive debate without dissention'.

[Paul's views on the importance of women remaining silent in church and his suggestion that they should ask their husbands later, if they require clarification – these are surely example parts of the Bible that tell us about 'political correctness' in the Roman era. They are ideas that need to be adjusted to suit the modern world of the twenty-first century.]

4.02.11: Chapter 15 (The Resurrection of Christ)

Paul stresses that to be saved, you need to hold firmly to his preaching: that Christ died for our sins 'according to the Scriptures, that he was buried and was raised again on the third day 'also according to the Scriptures'. Paul also states that Jesus appeared to himself (Paul).

[Note that 'dying for our sins' can be interpreted as applying to all Christian martyrs, starting with John the Baptist – they all sacrificed their lives to save us from our 'sins'.]

In verse 13, Paul makes it clear that in his view that, <u>'If there is no resurrection of the dead, then not even Christ has been raised. And if Christ has not been raised, our preaching is useless and so is your faith.'</u>

[Do *we need to hold this view today? I think there are many Christians today who see 'faith in Jesus' being mainly about following his teaching. They do not reject the Resurrection, but neither to they strongly believe in it. If it is true, they will know, eventually.*]

Paul adds (vs 21-29), 'For since death came through a man [Adam], the resurrection of the dead comes also through a man [Jesus]. For as in Adam all die, so in Christ all will be made alive.'

Then: 'the end will come, when he hands over the kingdom to God the Father, after he has destroyed all dominium, authority, and power.' And: 'The last enemy to be destroyed is death.'

Finally, 'the Son himself shall be made subject to him [God], so that God may be all in all.' *[Jesus submits to God.]*

Paul later imagines a Resurrection Body, which is spiritual and changed in a flash, in a twinkling of an eye, at the last trumpet.' (Vs 51,52)

[It is not clear to what extent Paul's thinking in verses 21-29, was generally supported by the Pharisees, or whether it was specifically Paul's contribution of Christian theology about 'Original Sin' and Adam and Eve.]

[Paul's opinions on what Christians should believe to attain salvation reflects his thinking some twenty years or so after Jesus' crucifixion. Is it reasonable to expect all people in the twenty-first century to believe things in the same way that Paul did?]

END OF NOTES ON *CORINTHIANS 1*

4.03: 2 CORINTHIANS

4.03.01: Chapter 1

V 3,4: 'Praise be to the God and Father of our Lord Jesus Christ, the Father of Compassion and the God of all comfort, who comforts us in all our troubles, so that we can comfort those in any trouble with the comfort we have received from God.'

Paul makes a clear that Jesus is the son of God in a way that does not imply that Jesus is God, as defined in the Nicene Creed, nearly 300 years later. As Paul sees it Jesus is given a high level of authority on earth by his Father, God. God comforts Christians in their troubles with a purpose; to give Christians an obligation to comfort others. This underpins Paul's view that any true Christian will demonstrate his belief in Jesus by how he treats and comforts others. *In other words, good works are a measure of faith in both God and Jesus.*

Ch 1:8,9: 'We were under great pressure, far beyond our ability to endure, . .' 'But this happened that we might not rely on ourselves but on God, who raises the dead. He has delivered us from such a deadly peril . . . as you help us by your prayers.'

This highlights the traditional Christian view that God is very active on earth and good things and bad that happen to people reflect the will of God ('he has delivered us'). Also, note the firm view that God may respond to prayers by Christians and take action to help people in distress (stop a ship from sinking or stop the earthquake?). [Do we see God acting in this direct way in 2022?]

4.03.02: Chapter 2 (Forgiveness of the Sinner)

V 5-8: This passage encourages Christian groups to forgive members who cause others grief, to recreate harmony in the group. Again, this is another example of Paul stressing how Christians should put their faith in practice. Christianity is as much about doing as about believing.

4.03.03: Chapter 3 (The Glory of the New Covenant)

The ministry of the Holy Spirit brings righteousness. 'Now the Lord is the Spirit, and where the Spirit of the Lord is, there is freedom.' (I assume that the Holy Spirit is God's motivating force within us.)

4.03.04: Chapter 4 (Treasures in Jars of Clay)

Our earthly bodies are visualized as jars of clay that contain the life-giving Holy Spirit: 'so that the life of Jesus may also be revealed in our body': by our works as we practice our faith.

A Christian life is a life of service: 'For we do not preach ourselves, but Jesus Christ as Lord, and ourselves as servants for Jesus' sake.'

Life after death: '. . . we know that the one who raised the Lord Jesus from the dead will also raise us with Jesus and present us with you in his presence': where God and Jesus will be seen. (This is how Paul saw it, 2000 years ago.)

4.03.05: Chapter 5 (Our Heavenly Dwelling)

Vs 7-10: 'We live by faith, not by sight.' 'For we must all appear before the judgment seat of Christ.'

Faith is *not* sight and this needs to be accepted. It is by what we think, say, and do, that we will have to answer for at Judgment Day.

[One does not have to believe in the certainty of 'Judgment Day' to be able to use the 'idea' of a Judgment Day as a 'litmus test' on one's thoughts, words, and actions.]

4.03.05b: Chapter 5 (The Ministry of Reconciliation)

Vs 11-20: 'Since, then, we know what it is to fear the Lord, we try to persuade men.'

Christ's love compels us to live not for ourselves but for him who died for them and was raised again. A Christian life is about 'doing' and service to others – not simply about 'believing' or worshipping.

'. . . if anyone is in Christ, he is a new creation.'

V21: 'God made him who had no sin to be sin for us, so that in him we might become the righteousness of God.'

This is a complex verse. It illustrates Paul's view that Jesus was not simply good: he was perfect. Secondly, Paul's believed that Jesus died to take away our sins, which implies that God needed human sins to be paid for (to be 'redeemed'), rather than simply be forgiven in accordance with Jesus' teaching. And thirdly, that by dying on the Cross, Jesus enabled Christians to become righteous in God's eyes.

[In 2022, Christians may need to unpick this verse and re-think how much they can accept or reject it. Why did God need a 'Redeemer' when Jesus (God with us?) taught the importance of forgiveness without conditions other than genuine repentance?]

4.03.06: Chapter 6

V 2: 'I tell you, now is the time of God's favour, now is the day of salvation.'

There seems to be no doubt that Paul anticipated the coming of the kingdom of God as something that would happen soon. *[How would he have reacted, had he known that it would not have come about after 2000 years?]*

4.03.07: Chapter 7

V 1: 'Since we have these promises, dear friends, let us purify ourselves from everything that contaminates body and spirit, perfecting holiness out of reverence for God.'

Paul stressed the importance of aiming for perfection in mind and body out of reverence for God, thus developing an attitude to God that followed from Hebrew traditions of worshipping God as a great king and judge. At the same time, Paul appeared to believe that a Christian who is inspired by the Holy Spirit would wish to offer their life in service to others because of his new mindset, rather than for fear of future judgment.

Paul writes in Ch 9, v11: 'Because of the service by which you have proved yourselves, men will praise God for the obedience that accompanies your confession of the Gospel of Christ.'

4.03.08: Chapter 11

Paul was very worried about false prophets. To justify his high standing as an apostle, he stressed in detail how he had suffered in his years of preaching the Gospel of Christ. (He had worked hard, been flogged, and beaten for his efforts, been imprisoned, shipwrecked, and in danger from bandits and gentiles.)

END OF NOTES ON 2 CORINTIHIANS

4.04: *GALATIANS*

4.04.01: Chapter 1

V 12: Paul called by God. 'I did not receive it from any man, nor was I taught it; rather, I received it by revelation from Jesus Christ.'

One does not want to challenge Paul's memory of events, but prior to his Damascus moment, as Saul of Tarsus, Paul spent an unspecified amount of time arresting and interrogating Christians on behalf of the Jewish authorities in Jerusalem. It is likely that over time, Saul heard repeated testimony from those he interrogated, covering their beliefs about the life, teaching, and death of Jesus and about his resurrection from the dead. After several months, Saul must have become an expert on the beliefs of these early Jewish Christians and the evidence of his later conversion suggests that he had been wrestling with his conscience for some time, before he had a breakdown through overwork or sunstroke on the road to Damascus, after which he believed Jesus spoke directly to him.

In Galatians, Paul explained how he went up to Jerusalem and met Peter and James, the brother of Jesus. He was gradually accepted by them. Fourteen years later, he returned to Jerusalem with Barnabas and Titus. He notes that Titus was not compelled to be circumcised. (Ch 2)

4.04.02: Chapter 2

V 7: Paul explained that he was entrusted with the task of preaching the gospel to the Gentiles, just as Peter had been to the Jews.

Later there is evidence of some disagreements between Paul and Peter over Gentiles having to follow all the Law and the Prophets and be circumcised. Paul argued that all were justified by faith in Jesus Christ and not by following Jewish Law. (2:16)

4.04.03: Chapter 3

This last subject is continued in Chapter 3, v 8: 'The Scripture foresaw that God would justify Gentiles by faith and announced the Gospel in advance to Abraham. "All nations will be blessed through you."'

(V 15) 'Christ redeemed us from the curse of the law by becoming a curse for us, for it is written, "Cursed is everyone who is hung from a tree."'

(V 26) 'You are all sons of God through faith in Christ Jesus.

(V 28) *'For there is neither Jew nor Greek, slave nor free, male nor female, you are all of one in Christ Jesus.'*

4.04.04: Chapter 4

(V 4) 'But when the time had fully come, God sent his Son, born of woman, born under law, to redeem those under law, that we might the full rights of sons.'

(Surely, Paul would have referred to the Virgin Birth, had he been aware of it?)

(4:6) 'God sent the Spirit of his Son into our hearts, the Spirit who calls out, "Abba, Father."'

4.04.05: Chapter 5 (Freedom in Christ)

(V 1) 'It is for freedom that Christ has set us free.'

(V 6) 'For in Christ Jesus neither circumcision nor uncircumcision has any value. The only thing that counts is faith expressing itself through love.'

Note that Ch 5:6 confirms that 'faith' needs to be measured by how one leads one's life. (It is not a stand-alone thing); it becomes a verb, a doing word, expressed in actions, through an attitude of love
(V 14) 'The entire law is summed up in a single command: "Love your neighbour as yourself."'

Life by the Spirit:

You will not gratify your sinful nature and involve yourself in sexual immorality; impurity; debauchery; idolatry; witchcraft; hatred; discord; jealousy; fits of rage; selfish ambition; dissensions; factions; envy; drunkenness; orgies and the like.

Life of the Spirit is love and is found as: joy; peace; patience; kindness; goodness; faithfulness; gentleness; self-control; and doing good to all; carrying each other's burden. *(Paul indicates that these will gain eternal life.)*

END OF THE NOTES ON GALATIONS

4.05: *EPHESIANS*

4.05.01: Chapter 1

The *New Bible Commentary* says that *Ephesians* 'is breathtaking in its theological grasp of the scope of God's purposes in Christ or the Church.'

Each of us needs to decide whether 'theological grasp' is better understood as 'the amazing imagination of St Paul, as he writes about God with such confidence in what are clearly Paul's own assumptions about the 'cosmic reconciliation in Christ.'

(V4) 'For he chose us in him before the creation of the world to be holy and blameless in his sight.'

There are different interpretations of this last verse, but it introduces the idea of 'predestination.' God is assumed to have known everything about the future, even before the creation of the universe – even who the 'elect' would be, and who would have eternal life in heaven. [*Where did Paul get this information: from others or in his dreams? These seem to be wild assumptions about the nature of God with no basis other than dreams or supernatural communications with God or angels. Do we need to take these suggestion as 'God-breathed' in 2022?*]

(V5) 'In love, he predestined us to be adopted as his sons through Jesus Christ, in accordance with his pleasure and will.'

These are assumptions by Paul.

(V7) 'In him we have redemption through his blood, the forgiveness of sins, in accordance with God's grace.'

Paul is developing the Christian idea of Jesus redeeming humanity by his death on the Cross and that God demanded a payment, which seems in conflict with Jesus' teaching that we should be prepared to forgive others who acknowledge they have done wrong. *Why would God, then, wish a payment for forgiving sins that are a consequence of human nature over which humans have no control?*

(V11, 12) 'In him we were also chosen, having been predestined according to the plan of him who works out everything in conformity with the purpose of his will in order that we, who were the first to hope in Christ, might be for the praise of his glory.'

This is more on the theme of predestination.

(V13, 14) Paul suggests that having been saved, you were marked in him with a seal, the promised Holy Spirit, who is a deposit guaranteeing our inheritance until the redemption of those who are God's possession – to the praise of his glory.'

[*This is surely imaginative thinking, designed to reassure the Ephesian Christians?*]

(Vs 19, 20) Paul describes the Holy Spirit as like the working of God's 'mighty strength, which he exerted in Christ when he raised him from the dead and seated him on God's right hand in the heavenly realms.'

[*This confirms Paul's absolute conviction that God raised Jesus from the dead and he imagines Jesus sat at God's right hand in heaven. This does not seem to me to be in full agreement with the Nicene Creed image of God, Jesus, and the Holy Spirit – being of one substance; it is more as assertion of the original belief of the disciples that Jesus would one day sit at the right hand of his Father, under the authority of God.*

(Vs22,23) 'And God placed all things under his feet and appointed him to be head over everything for the church, which is his body, the fulness of him who fills everything in every way.'

This does not seem to be Jesus who is speaking. Rather, it is evidence that ideas about who Jesus was evolved in the decades following the crucifixion.]

4.05.02: Chapter 2 (Made Alive in Jesus)

(V3,4,5) Paul says that 'All of us also live . . . gratifying our sinful nature and following its desires and thoughts.' But, because of his great love for us, God, who is rich in mercy made us alive with Christ even when we were dead in transgressions – it is by grace you have been saved.' He adds in verses 8-10, 'through faith – and this not from yourselves, it is a gift from God – not by works, so that no-one can boast.'

Underlying the above passage is Paul's idea that God is justifiably angry with humanity.

Paul explains that previously Gentiles were excluded from God's covenants with Israel, but now, through Jesus Christ, Gentiles 'have been brought near by the blood of Christ.' Through the Holy Spirit, Gentiles have now access to the Father God.

[*The logic here follows from Paul's sincere belief that everything in Ancient Hebrew Scripture had fulfilment in Jesus Christ. He could not imagine, for example, that Jesus' teaching and philosophy of love was a revolutionary new import into Jewish thinking that came in after the end of the Babylonian Exile and was strongly influenced by the Persian religion at the time of Cyrus the Great. This phenomenon was discounted in the Classical world because 'newness' or 'original thinking' was looked down upon, whereas 'the ancient provenance of ideas,' and prophecy, were greatly respected. But the reality is that there is an irreconcilable chasm between the angry God of Moses and the loving God of Jesus.*]

4.05.03: Chapter 3 (Paul the Preacher to the Gentiles)

Here Paul reviews how by revelation by Christ he was called to preach to the Gentiles.

He prays for the Ephesians that the Holy Spirit dwell in their hearts through faith.

4.05.04: Chapter 4 (Unity in the Body of Christ)

Paul urges that the Ephesians will have a life worthy of the calling they have received. They should be completely humble, patient, and be loving towards one another, with one Lord, one faith and one baptism,

Jesus ascended to the heavens after he had descended to earth and gives different gifts to his followers – to be apostles, or prophets, pastors, or teachers – all who make up the body of Christ, working in unity, speaking the truth in love. Paul writes that they will not be like the Gentiles who give themselves over to sensuality, impurity, with a lust for more. Christians must put off falsehood, speak truthfully, love to their neighbour, steal no longer, work and do something useful with their own hands, share with people in need, avoid unwholesome talk, be constructive in speech, avoid bitterness, rage, anger, brawling, slander, malice, and be compassionate and forgiving with others, imitating the life of Jesus Christ.

(The emphasis here is on living a Christian life; putting faith into practice.)

4.05.05: Chapter 5

This continues the theme of leading a loving and constructive life.

We should all try to be wise and make the most of every moment. Do not get drunk or become involved in debauchery. Be filled with the Holy Spirit and speak to one another with psalms, hymns, and spiritual songs. Give thanks to the God the Father for everything in the name of Jesus Christ.

Wives are asked to submit to their husbands (which reflects the social norms of the period). Husbands are asked to love their wives, as they love themselves and the wife must respect their husband.

(V29) A parallel is drawn here between a man loving his wife and Christ loving his church, and the metaphor has since used or abused by the Church. (It is a useful subject for further discussion.)

4.05.06: Chapter 6

Children are told to honour and obey their parents. And parents (fathers) are told not to exasperate their children.

Slaves are asked to obey their masters and serve them wholeheartedly. *This may confuse many people in the twenty-first century. One needs to understand that Christianity developed in the Roman world, where slavery was a fact of normal life for a great proportion of the population. The early church was helpless and could do nothing to change this, without being totally rejected by civil authorities. It was completely revolutionary of them to teach that in God's eyes there was no slave versus free persons, and no distinction between men and women.*

Hence, masters (and mistresses) were told to treat their slaves with compassion.

Paul ends the letter to the Galations with a bucketful of metaphors, designed to motivate them to move forward in life with the Holy Spirit. They are told:

to put on the armour of God against the devil;
to stand firm with the belt of truth about them;
to take up the shield of faith to defend themselves;
to put on the breastplate of righteousness;
to take up the helmet of salvation;
and the sword of the Spirit, which is the Word of God.

These are all concerned with a willingness to work and to fight to defend and promote Christianity day by day, living the

Christian life. The focus is not church worship or prayer, except as a promoter of Christian fellowship and an energising spirit of thankfulness among Christians.

END OF NOTES ON EPHESIANS

4.06: *PHILIPPIANS*

4.06.01: Chapter 1

(Vs9-11) 'And this is my prayer: that your love may abound more and more in knowledge and depth of insight, so that you may be able to discern what is best and may be pure and blameless until the day of Christ, filled with the fruit of righteousness that comes through Jesus Christ – to the glory and praise of God.'

[*Here, Paul indicates three key points. First that Christians must live a life that is pure and blameless inspired by the teaching of Jesus 'until the day of Christ.' This reflects a second point: that the Second Coming of Jesus on earth was 'imminent' (not in more than two thousand years in the future). Thirdly, Paul clearly separates Jesus and God, with Jesus being lesser than God (and quite different from the later Nicene image, three hundred years later).*]

(V13) Several times Paul refers to being 'in chains for Christ'. I presume this refers to his period as a prisoner in Rome.

4.06.02: Chapter 2

(V2-4) Paul urges the Philippians to be like-minded in love and look after the interests of others. *(Again emphasizing 'living the Christian life, day to day.)*

(V9-11) This is a famous passage about Jesus humbling himself as a servant, obedient to death on a cross and saying that 'God exalted him' and that 'at the name of Jesus, every knee should bow . . . to the glory of God the Father.' *(Is this another clear image of Jesus as lesser than God?)*

(V12) The Christian life: 'Do everything without complaining or arguing' to set an example to others in society.

4.06.03: Chapter 3

(V19) Christians 'eagerly await' Jesus Christ as the 'Saviour from heaven.'

4.06.04: Chapter 4

Paul ends by urging the Philippians to pray and petition to God with thankfulness and do, always, what is noble, what is right, pure, lovely, and admirable, and to put in to practice all that they have learned from him (and one assumes also, from Jesus). Again, this is a focus on living the Christian life, day to day and setting a good example to others of what a Christian life is like.

END OF NOTES ON PHILIPPIANS

4.07: *COLOSSIANS*

4.07.01: Chapter 1

Paul reminded the Colossians that they must give thanks to God the Father who has rescued them from the dominium of darkness and brought them into the kingdom of the Son he loves, in whom they have redemption, the forgiveness of sins.

4.07.02: Chapter 2

Jesus is the 'image of the invisible God, the firstborn of all creation', and by him 'all things were created: things in heaven and on earth, visible and invisible, whether thrones or powers or rulers or authorities: all things were created by him and for him.' Jesus is 'the head of the church and the firstborn from among the dead, so that in everything he might have supremacy.' Paul adds: 'For God was pleased to have all his fulness dwell' in Jesus, and through 'him to reconcile to himself all things, whether things on earth or things in heaven, by making peace through his blood, shed on the cross.'

[*Note that here is the fullest description so far, provided by Paul of how he sees Jesus, and one can understand how at the Council of Nicaea many bishops could be persuaded that Jesus was indeed 'of one substance with the Father.'*

The question in 2022, is whether Paul's vision of Jesus was based upon his imagined meeting with Jesus, maybe in a dream, at or after his conversion? On what other authority did Paul decide that Jesus has existed since the 'beginning of time' and that he has all the authority that Paul sees in Jesus? Those who see the Holy Bible as 'God-breathed' may accept Paul's assessment of Jesus; others who believe that the Bible was put together by imperfect humans, inspired by tales of Jesus, may have alternative viewpoints about Jesus' status. Who is right?]

Paul urges the Colossians to embrace this 'mystery of God, namely Christ, in whom are hidden all the treasures of wisdom and knowledge.' (2:1-5) [This for me seems an excellent way to imagine Jesus and God, because God will always remain as the ultimate mystery behind Creation – a mystery that is totally beyond the experience and ability to conceive of by the human brain. To say that we see God in Jesus is enough. That is as far as our 'definition' needs to go. Jesus provides a 'human' image; he is evoked as a real person, a teacher, a guru, and many of his words have been recorded for us to think about. The Holy Spirit is the motivating force within us.]

(2:9) 'For in Christ all the fulness of the Deity lives in bodily form.' God raised Jesus from the dead (v12), having accepted the death of Jesus as the redemption price of the "Original Sins" of human beings.' *[This is how Paul saw things.]* Paul wrote that God nailed our sins to the cross.

In verses 16 to 17, Paul suggests, 'Therefore do not let anyone judge you by what you eat and drink, or regarding a religious festival, a New Moon celebration, or a Sabbath Day.' *Here Paul seems to be saying that how you worship is of minor importance against leading your life in accordance with the teachings of Jesus.*

[This has major implications in a multi-cultural and scientific society. We are called to respect others with similar values to ourselves, not to withdraw into an elite sect.]

4.07.03: Chapter 3

(Vs5-16) Put to death, therefore, whatever belongs to your earthly nature: sexual immorality, impurity, lust, evil desires, greed, and idolatry. Get rid of anger, rage, malice, slander, and filthy language. Clothe yourself with compassion, kindness, humility, gentleness, and patience. Bear with each other and forgive grievances against others, put on love, and live in perfect unity, singing psalms, hymns and spiritual songs. *Do these things in the 'name of the Lord Jesus, giving thanks to God the Father through him.' [This is the essential consequence, as Paul sees it, of having a genuine 'faith.']*

(Vs 18-24) Additional rules are set down for Christian households. Wives should submit to husbands, husbands should love their wives, fathers should not embitter their children, slaves should willingly obey their earthly masters (because the early church could do nothing about slavery in the Roman world) and masters should treat their slaves kindly. Constant prayer is advocated.

END OF NOTES ON COLOSSIANS

4.08: *1 THESSALONIANS*

4.08.01: Chapter 1

Greetings.

4.08.02: Chapter 2

(V15) There is an unfortunate reference to the 'Jews who killed the Lord Jesus', when it should read 'the authorities' or 'Jewish authorities'.

4.08.03: Chapter 4

(Vs 3-12) It is God's will that you should be sanctified: that you should avoid sexual immorality, that each of you should learn to control his own body in a way that is holy and honourable, not in passionate lust. . .' 'Make it your own business to work with your own hands . . . so that your daily life may win the respect of outsiders. '[*Again, there is an emphasis upon 'faith' being validated or expressed, by 'doing', putting faith into practice,' or by personal hard work with one's hands.*]

(Vs 16-18) '. . the Lord [Jesus] will come down from heaven, with a loud command, with the voice of the archangel, and with the trumpet call of God, and the dead in Christ will rise first. After that, we who are still alive and are left will be caught up together with them in the clouds to meet the Lord in the air. And so, we will be with the Lord forever.'
[This is how Paul imagined the end would be.]

4.08.04: Chapter 5

(V 2) '. . the day of the Lord will come like a thief in the night
. .'

(V 8) '.. be self-controlled, putting on faith and love as a breastplate, and the hope of salvation as helmet.'

(Vs 12-22) '. . respect those who work hard among you.' '.. warn those who are idle, encourage the timid, help the weak, be patient with everyone. Make sure that nobody pays back wrong for wrong, but always try to be kind to each other and everyone else.' 'Be joyful always, pray continually, give thanks . .' 'Hold on to the good. Avoid every kind of evil.' [*Christianity is a verb - it demands application.*]

END OF NOTES ON 1 THESSALONIANS

4.09: 2 THESSALONIANS

4.09.01: Chapter 1

(V1) 'We boast about your perseverance and faith in all the persecutions and trials you are enduring.'

Paul suggests that God will 'pay back trouble to those who trouble them' and 'give relief to those who are troubled.' Those who do not 'believe' will be punished with everlasting destruction. *[Do Christians still have to believe this?]*

4.09.02: Chapter 2

Thessalonians should watch out for false prophets about Jesus' Second Coming.

4.09.03: Chapter 3

Warnings against idleness. Paul reminds them that when he was there, he was not idle: he worked day and night to avoid being a burden on them and paid for food he received. Paul says: 'If a man will not work, he shall not eat.' *[Christianity is about helping others.]*

END OF NOTES ON 2 THESSALONIANS

4.10: *1 TIMOTHY*

4.10.01: Chapter 1

Paul warns about false teachers offering 'myths and endless genealogies', that promote 'controversies', rather than God's work which is by faith. (*What about the genealogy in Matthew?*)

(V15) 'Christ Jesus came into the world to save sinners.'

[*The essential here is identifying the meaning of 'sin' and to correct it in one's way of life.*]

4.10.02: Chapter 2

Prayers and thanks should be offered for everyone, including kings and all those in authority to ensure that all may live peaceful lives.

[*Christians must live law-abiding lives even when they have no say in how they are governed. They must be good citizens, live peaceful, quiet and godly lives.*]

God wants all to be saved. Christ Jesus 'gave himself as a ransom for all men.'

[*Is this a call for new approaches in a multi-cultural society, engaging with any other groups that have similar values to Christians, and to identify 'goodness' wherever it can be found in society? Rather than being a closed community, focusing on worship?*]

[The subject of Jesus giving himself as a redeemer and paying a ransom, has been discussed previously in these notes.]

(V9-15) A woman should dress 'modestly with decency and propriety, not with braided hair or gold or pearls or expensive clothes, but with good deeds, appropriate for women who profess to worship God.' 'A woman should learn in quietness and full submission.' Note that Paul does not permit a woman to teach or have authority over a man; she must be silent. He explains: 'For Adam was formed first, then Eve.' 'But women will be saved through childbearing, if they continue in faith, love and holiness with propriety.'

[These above statements need unpicking, as elsewhere Paul acknowledged the valuable contribution of women in evangelism and one woman is named as an apostle. These recommendations follow social norms in the Roman period. Any other ideas about men versus women would have been ridiculed.]

4.10.03: Chapter 3

Overseers and deacons.

Christian overseers and deacons must be above reproach, with one wife, be temperate, self-controlled, respectable, hospitable, able to teach, not given to drunkenness, gentle, not quarrelsome, not a lover of money. He must manage his family well and see that his children obey him and give him proper respect. He must not be a recent convert.

4.10.04: Chapter 4

Everything that God created is good. Christians should set an example in life, in love, in faith and in purity. They will devote themselves to 'Scripture', to preaching, to teaching.

4.10.05: Chapter 5 (Advice about Widows and Elders)

All should 'put their religion into practice by caring for others, starting with their own family and repaying debts to their own parents and grandparents.'

Young widows are counselled to marry, to have children and manage their homes.

Elders should be respected.

4.10.06: Chapter 6

Slaves should respect their masters (and mistresses) regardless of whether they are, or are not, of the faith.

The love of money is the root of all kinds of evil.

The rich should be generous and willing to share their wealth with others.

END OF NOTES ON 1 TIMOTHY

4.11: *2 TIMOTHY*

4.11.01: Chapter 1

Do not be ashamed to testify about the Lord.
Grace was given us in Christ before the beginning of time.
Keep the pattern of sound teaching, with faith and love in Christ Jesus, and all that Paul had said to them.

4.11.02: Chapter 2

Endure hardship with us like a good soldier of Christ Jesus.
Christ Jesus was raised from the dead. He was descended from David.

[The first assertion was a firm belief by Paul, the apostles, and the earliest Christians; it provided evidence of life after death and the kingdom of God. The second assertion linked Jesus to the history of the ancient Hebrews. It seems to have been accepted, though, at best, Jesus was the adopted son of Joseph and Jesus' father was the Holy Spirit. [Was Jesus the Son of David or the Son of God?]

Don't be quarrelsome. Avoid godless chatter. Pursue righteousness, faith, love, and peace, be kind to everyone, teach the word and do not be resentful. *[Faith will be evident in the lives of Christians.]*

4.11.03: Chapter 3

Paul is rather bitter and warns that there will be godlessness in the 'Last Days'. *[Is this genuine 'prophecy' or Paul's despondency coming to the fore?]*

4.11.04: Chapter 4

Paul speaks of having fought the good fight and having finished the race.

END OF NOTES ON 2 TIMOTHY

4.12: *TITUS*

4.12.01: Chapter 1

'Paul . . . an apostle of Jesus Christ or the faith of God's elect and the knowledge of the truth that leads to godliness – a faith and knowledge resting on the hope of eternal life, which God, who does not lie, promised before the beginning of time.'

Titus' Task on Crete:

Paul identifies the qualities required in an elder of the Christian Church: An elder must be blameless, the husband of but one wife, a man whose children believe and are not open to the charge of being wild and disobedient – not overbearing, not quick-tempered, not given to drunkenness, not violent, not pursuing dishonest gain. Rather he must be hospitable, one who does what is good, who is self-controlled, upright, holy, and disciplined. He must hold firmly to the trustworthy message he has been taught . . .'

Cretans are urged to pay 'no attention to Jewish myths.'

Paul speaks of those who 'claim to know God, but by their actions they deny him.' [*This endorses the idea that a Christian's faith is demonstrated by their actions.*]

4.12.02: Chapter 2

'Teach the older men to be temperate, worthy of respect, self-controlled, and sound in faith, in love and endurance. Likewise teach older women to be reverent in the way they live . . . they can train the younger women to love their husbands and children, to be self-controlled and pure, to be busy at home, to be kind, and to be subject to their husbands, . . Similarly, encourage the young men to be self-controlled . . . doing what is good. In your teaching show integrity, seriousness, and soundness of speech . . . Teach slaves to be subject to their masters in everything . . . For the Grace of God that brings salvation has appeared to all men. It teaches us to say "No" to ungodliness and worldly passions, and to live self-controlled, upright and godly lives in this present age, while we wait for the blessed hope – the glorious appearing of our great God and Saviour, Jesus Christ, . . .' *[This is more emphasis on what it means to be a Christian, in terms of lifestyle and Christian witness.]*

4.12.03: Chapter 3

Chapter 3 reminds people to be subject to rulers and to authorities, to be obedient and ready to do whatever is good, to slander no-one, to be peaceable and considerate, and to show humility towards all men.'

Paul's final remarks:

Paul writes that he has 'to winter there' (at Nicopolis). (This indicates that he was not yet a prisoner in Rome.)

END OF NOTES ON TITUS

4.13: *PHILEMON*

4.13.01: Chapter 1

'Paul, a prisoner of Jesus Christ, and Timothy our brother.'

Paul refers to Onesimus who is 'no longer a slave, but better than a slave, as a dear brother' who Paul is sending to those to whom the letter is addressed.

Paul asks them to prepare a guest room for himself, as he hopes to be released soon.

END OF NOTES ON PHILEMON

4.14: *HEBREWS*

Reference to Chapters 1, 9, 10, 12, and 13:

4.14.01: Chapter 1

'The Son Superior to Angels.'

'In the past God spoke to our forefathers through the prophets at many times and in many ways, but in these last days he has spoken to us by his Son, whom he appointed heir of all things, <u>and through whom he made the universe.</u>' 'The Son is the radiance of God's glory and the exact representation of his being . . .' 'After he had provided purification for sins, he sat down at the right hand side of the Majesty in heaven. So, he became as much superior to the angels, as the name he has inherited is superior to theirs.'

[It is difficult to imagine on what authority the writer of Hebrews can be certain of his idea of who Jesus is, in relation to God, even though he finds quotations from Ancient Hebrew Scripture to support his views. Are these in turn, wild imaginings of what God is like?]

Later, in Chapter 5, the writer imagines Jesus being heard by God 'because of his reverent submission' and describes Jesus as 'designed by God to be high priest in the order of Melchizedek.'

[Either way Jesus appears to be imagined as lesser than God.]

Hebrews continues as a somewhat rambling imagining of Jesus being like the ancient Hebrew High Priest, Melchizedek at the time of Abraham.

4.14.02: Ch 9

'When Christ came as high priest of the good things, he went through the greater and more perfect tabernacle that is not mam-made.' 'For this reason, Christ is the mediator of a new covenant . . . now that he has died as a ransom to set them free from the sins committed under the first covenant.'

Referring to Old Testament traditions, the writer proclaims that 'without the shedding of blood there is no forgiveness.'

[This seems to me as though the writer is putting limits on what God can do! Why did Jesus need to die to pay for human sins? Why could not God have simply decided to forgive these 'original sins' or 'sins of human nature' and put in practice the advice that Jesus was giving everybody – always to forgive, to turn the other cheek, not to demand vengeance?]

The writer concludes that 'Christ was sacrificed once to take away the sins of many people; and he will appear a second time, not to bear sin, but to bring salvation to those who are waiting for him.'

4.14.03: Chapter 10

'. . . we have been made holy through the sacrifice of the body of Jesus Christ once for all.' *[Further stress on the idea that Jesus died as a redeemer of our sins.]*

4.14.04: Chapter 12

'Endure hardship as discipline.' 'No discipline seems pleasant at the time, but painful. Later on, however, it produces a harvest of righteousness and peace for those who have been trained by it.'

[Given regular persecution by local authorities and Jewish communities, Christians were encouraged to see hardship as sent by God to test their faith. Soon, many Christians started to see the Christian life in terms of hardship and suffering.]

'Make every effort to live in peace with all men and to be holy; without holiness no-one will see the Lord.' *[Maintaining a belief in unselfish love was a key objective.]*

4.14.05: Chapter 13

'Marriage should be honoured by all . . . for God will judge the adulterer and all the sexually immoral. Keep your lives free from the love of money and be content with what you have . . .' *[More teaching about leading a Christian life.]*

[Note: Hebrews is built around the belief that Jesus died on the Cross and paid God for the sins of the world.]

END OF NOTES ON HEBREWS

4.15: JAMES

4.15.01: Chapter 1

From James to 'the twelve tribes scattered among the nations.'
[This reference to the twelve tribes is ambiguous. It could mean members of the Jewish tribes, or it could indicate that the Gentiles were the inheritors of God's grace under a new Covenant from God, following the crucifixion of Jesus.]
'Everyone should be quick to listen, slow to speak and slow to become angry.'

'Religion that our God our Father accepts as pure and faultless is this: to look after orphans and widows in their distress and keep oneself from being polluted by the world.'

[The last two paragraphs emphasise the need to put 'faith' into practice.]

4.15.02: Chapter 2

'.. don't show favouritism.'

'Love your neighbour as yourself . . .'

'For whoever keeps the whole law and yet stumbles at just one point is guilty of breaking it all.' *[Rather an extreme view?]*

'Mercy triumphs over judgment.' *[A more important point than the past one?]*

'What good is it, my brothers, if a man claims to have faith, but has no deeds?' '. . . faith by itself, if not accompanied by action, is dead.' *[The key point. Christianity is about 'doing' and making a better world.]*

4.15.03: Chapter 3

The human tongue: 'It is a restless evil, full of deadly poison.'

'Who is wise and understanding among you? <u>Let him show it by his good life, by deeds done in the humility that comes from wisdom.</u>'

'But the wisdom that comes from heaven is first of all pure; then peace-loving, considerate, submissive, full of mercy and good fruit, impartial and sincere. Peacemakers who sow in peace raise a harvest of righteousness.'

[More on 'doing'.]

4.15.04: Chapter 4

'. . . friendship with the world is hatred towards God.' [Do not love the bad values of this world: material gain, vanity, etc.]

'Humble yourself before the Lord and he will lift you up.'

'. . . brothers, do not slander one another.'

When thinking of the future, adopt a philosophical stand: 'If it is the Lord's will, we will live and do this or that.'

4.15.05: Chapter 5

This starts with warnings to the rich to be careful how they use their wealth.

Christians are told to 'Be patient . . . until the Lord's coming.' '. . . be patient and stand firm, because the Lord's coming is near.'

'Don't grumble against each other, or you will be judged. The judge is standing at the door.' '. . . we consider blessed those who have persevered.'

'. . . do not swear [oaths]' 'Let your "Yes" be yes and your "No" , no . . .'

END OF NOTES ON JAMES

4.16: *1 PETER*

4.16.01: Chapter 1

'To God's elect, strangers to the world, . . . who have been chosen according to the fore-knowledge of God the Father, through the sanctifying work of the Spirit, for obedience to Jesus Christ and sprinkling by his blood.' '. . . he has given us new birth into a living hope through the resurrection of Jesus Christ from the dead . . .'

'Therefore, prepare your minds for action; be self-controlled; set your hope fully on the grace to be given to you when Jesus Christ is revealed.' [At the Second Coming.]

You were 'redeemed from the empty way of life handed down to you from your forefathers . . . with the precious blood of Christ, a lamb without blemish or defect. He was chosen before the creation of the world but was revealed in these last times for your sake.'

[In many of the letters, the status of Jesus is being upgraded, by speculation, such as Jesus being 'chosen before the Creation.' Jesus might have been chosen this way, but how can the Gospel writers have discovered this, except through dreams of God speaking to them?]

4.16.02: Chapter 2

Therefore, rid yourself of all malice and all deceit, hypocrisy, envy, and slander of every kind. Like newborn babies, crave pure spiritual milk.'

'Submit yourselves for the Lord's sake to every authority instituted among men: whether to the king, as supreme authority, or to governors, who are sent by him to punish those who do wrong and to commend those who do right. For it is God's will that by doing good you should silence the ignorant talk of foolish men.' '. . . live as servants of God. Show proper respect to everyone: Love the brotherhood of believers, fear-God, honour the king.'

'Slaves, submit yourselves to your masters with all respect, not only to those who are good and considerate, but also to those who are harsh.' 'Christ suffered for you, leaving you an example, that you should follow in his steps.' 'He committed no sin, and no deceit was found in his mouth.'

[Early Christians expected Jesus to return very soon. They expected that they would have no opportunity to change how society was organized. How do we see this advice two thousand years on?]

4.16.03: Chapter 3

'Wives . . . be submissive to your husbands so that they may be won over by the behaviour of their wives.' 'Husbands . . . be considerate as you live with your wives, and treat them with respect as the weaker partner . . .'

'Finally, all of you, live in harmony with one another; be sympathetic, love as brothers, be compassionate and humble. Do not repay evil with evil or insult with insult, but with blessing, because to this you were called so that you may inherit a blessing.'

'It is better, if it is God's will, to suffer for doing good than for doing evil.'

<u>Peter recalls Noah and the ark and says that even if only eight were saved through water, this water symbolizes baptism that now saves you also</u> – not the removal of dirt from your body but the pledge of a good conscience towards God. It saves you by the resurrection of Jesus Christ, who has gone to heaven and is at God's right hand – with angels, authorities and powers in submission to him.'

[Note above, the cleansing symbolism of baptism and the image of Jesus sitting in the place of honour at God's right hand. This is not the Nicene Creed image of Jesus. Peter imagines an early return of Jesus and no reorganization of society to create a fairer one.]

4.16.04: Chapter 4

'Therefore, since Christ suffered in body, arm yourself with the same attitude.'

Do not be like pagans and indulge in 'debauchery, lust, drunkenness, orgies, carousing and detestable idolatry.'

<u>'The end of all things is near.'</u>

'. . . be clear minded and self-controlled . . . Above all, love each other deeply, because love covers a multitude of sins. Offer hospitality to one another without grumbling. Each one should use whatever gift he has received to serve others, faithfully administering God's grace in its various forms.'

'...if you suffer as a Christian, do not be ashamed, but praise God that you bear that name.'

4.16.05: Chapter 5

'Be shepherds of God's flock.' Do not be 'greedy for money, but eager to serve; not lording it over those entrusted to you but being examples to the flock.'

Young men . . . be submissive to those who are older.' 'Be self-controlled and alert.'

END OF NOTES ON 1 PETER

4.17: *2 PETER*

4.17.01: Chapter 1

May you 'participate in the divine nature and escape corruption in the world caused by evil desires.' '. . . make every effort to add to your faith goodness; and to goodness, knowledge; and to knowledge, self-control, perseverance; and to perseverance, godliness; and to godliness kindness; and to kindness, love.'

Peter says that if they do these things, they will receive a rich welcome in the kingdom of heaven. *[Does this imply that those who do these things without any thought of reward, as non-Christians, may receive even greater rewards in heaven?]*

4.17.02: Chapter 2

Peter warns about false teachers. He says these will be condemned: 'For God did not spare his angels when they sinned, but sent them to hell, putting them into gloomy dungeons to be held for judgment.'

[Is this Peter offering his view of God and God's judgment? Where does forgiveness figure in Peter's thinking?]

The rest of Chapter 2 continues in a similar vein about 'continuing punishment' to offenders. He writes that the 'Blackest darkness is reserved for them.'

4.17.03: Chapter 3

Peter writes that in the Last Days, 'scoffers will come.' 'But the day of the Lord will come like a thief. The heavens will disappear with a roar; the elements will be destroyed by fire, and the earth and everything in it will be laid bare.' 'But in keeping with his promise, we are looking forward to a new heaven and a new earth, the home of righteousness.'

END OF NOTES ON 2 PETER

4.18: *1 JOHN*

4.18.01: Chapter 1

'God is light; in him there is no darkness at all.' 'But if we walk in the light, as he is in the light, we have fellowship with one another, and the blood of Jesus, his Son, purifies us from all sin.'

'If we claim to be without sin, we deceive ourselves and the truth is not in us.' *[This is a higher truth linked to our human nature.]*

'If we confess our sins, he is faithful and just and will forgive us our sins . . .' *[This is an article of traditional Christian faith.]*

4.18.02: Chapter 2

Jesus is 'the atoning sacrifice for our sins, and not only for ours, but for the sins of the whole world.'

These words confirm the belief of early Christians that Jesus was our redeemer; his death paid God for our sins.

[Is it necessary for ALL of us to believe this today? Can we not simply understand that Jesus died for his cause – his belief in the love of God and the power of forgiveness. Why was it necessary for Jesus' death to be interpreted as a sacrificial act, when God (logically) could have followed Jesus' teaching and simply forgiven ALL who sincerely repent of their sins?]

[Perhaps the answer lies in the mindset of St Paul and other apostles, who interpreted Jesus' death as explained by the history of the Ancient Hebrews, where blood of a sacrificial 'lamb' was necessary for forgiveness? This was how they saw it. Do we need to see it in the same way in 2022?]

'Whosoever claims to live in him must walk as Jesus did.' *[This makes good sense. One's faith is illustrated by how one lives.]*

'Anyone who claims to be in the light but hates his brother is still in the darkness.' [Here 'brother' equates to 'neighbour' or 'anyone we deal with.]

'Do not love the world or anything in the world.'

John warns that 'this is the last hour' during which the 'antichrist' is coming. *[This confirms that much in the gospels needs to be interpreted in the light of an expectation that Jesus' Second Coming and Final Judgment were imminent. All the advice in the Gospels and Letter is linked to this certainty in their mind.]*

The antichrist *'denies that Jesus is the Christ.'* *[This seems very clear, but with faith in Jesus, the apostles believed that there had to be a dramatic transformation of values that would be revealed in how one lived.]*

[Now, 2000 years later, should we all be focusing on Jesus' teaching and his gospel of love and forgiveness to build better communities here and now, and maybe, save the planet?]

Does Peter understand this when he writes: 'If you know that he is righteous, you know that <u>everyone who does what is right has been born of him.</u>' *[Does this relate to everyone and not just Christians or Jews?]*

The following statements from have universal application:

'No-one who continues to sin has either seen him or known him.'

'Anyone who does not do what is right is not a child of God.'

'We should love one another.'

'. . . we should lay down our life for our brothers.'

'If anyone has material possessions and sees his brother in need but has no pity on him, how can the love of God be in him? Dear children, let us not love with words and tongues but with actions and in truth.'

4.18.03: Chapter 4

Peter emphasises that believing in Jesus as Christ is critical, but elsewhere we are taught that few of us will be saved by our own efforts, and that we will be saved by the grace of God.

Surely a loving God will identify with unselfish love, regardless of what we call ourselves? This must be why Peter writes: 'Whoever does not love does not know God. God is love.' Peter repeats this several times.

Peter believed that God showed his love by sending his son into this world and that Jesus died to pay for our sins. Many Christians still adhere firmly to this idea.

4.18.04: Chapter 5

Peter concludes that 'God's commands are not burdensome,' in themselves – though people who do good may find themselves in danger from time to time – but unselfish love is rewarding to those who have this mindset.

[This is why those who believe that suffering is a necessary part of a Christian life have lost the plot. It can be that Christians may suffer, but Jesus only taught love and forgiveness. Christians can enjoy life as much as non-Christians.]

'He who has the Son has life; he who does not have the Son of God does not have life.'

[One can wholeheartedly accept this last assertion, assuming that 'having' the Son is more about being motivated by unselfish love, rather than simply believing who Jesus was

or is. The litmus test for judgment is belief in action. There have been endless numbers of sincere 'Christians' in history who have lived lives motivated by selfishness and hatred of others.]

END OF NOTES ON 1 JOHN

4.19: 2 JOHN

To the 'chosen lady' and others.

'I ask you to love one another.'

Beware of the antichrist: 'Anyone who runs ahead and does not continue in the teaching of Christ does not have God.'

[Note the emphasis on "the teaching of Christ".]

END OF THE NOTES ON 2 JOHN

4.20: *3 JOHN*

To Gaius.
The author speaks of problems among local Christians.
He hopes to be with them soon.

END OF NOTES ON 3 JOHN

4.21: *JUDE*

Jude refers to 'godless men, who change the grace of our God into a license for immorality and deny Jesus Christ, our only Sovereign and Lord.

Jude warns against following false teaching and asks readers of the letter to persevere.

END OF NOTES ON JUDE

*

REFLECTIONS

The Holy Bible becomes the more amazing and inspiring the more one examines it.

The last thing that is needed is for some group to come along and insist that the Bible (Old or New Testament) is re-written to accord with the political correctness of the Western world of the twenty-first century.

The New Testament reveals the mindset of the Roman world of two thousand years ago, while the Old Testament reveals concepts about God and uses the poetic language of earlier periods in Jewish history.

Any attempt to re-edit the Bible will give a false impression of what the writers of the Old and New Testament were saying, because what they were saying can only be properly interpreted if we understand their evolving visions of history, Creation, and God.

The New Testament still maintains the ancient vision of a three-tiered universe, with heaven above the canopy of the stars. In this vision, the earth is flat, not round, and the fiery regions of Hades or Hell lie beneath our feet. Time is measured in centuries, and Creation is believed to have occurred maybe six thousand years ago. Adam was the first human.

Thus, when God created Eve from Adam, he established a hierarchy of gender.

Regarding illness and death, these were understood to be a consequence of the disobedience of Adam and Eve in the Garden of Eden: illness and death are caused by 'sin'.

The sinful nature of 'man' explained why the earth is in a mess.

The New Testament describes a world where the strong oppress the weak, where despotism and institutions, such as slavery, are such normal aspects of life as to be considered permanent features, until a new, everlasting kingdom of God is created, either here on earth or up in heaven.

We are told that in heaven, there will no longer be divisions such as male or female, slave versus free people, or married versus single – and all the evils that are associated with sex (in all its manifestations) will no longer exist.

All these 'truths' were believed to have been prophesied in the Bible, since the beginning of time.

There are still many Christians who maintain this ancient mindset in the twenty-first century, but I think most modern Christians can read any passage in the Bible and understand that, today, we need to re-interpret some things in the Bible metaphorically.

We now know that Creation occurred millions of years ago. Human nature is a consequence of the slow evolution of species, and illness and death are caused by accidents, criminal activity, viruses, and infections, rather than by demons and evil spirits or the disobedience of Adam and Eve.

The laws of physics now explain phenomena, rather than magic and superstition. And emerging democratic ideas inform us about sexual equality, gender issues, and lesbian/homosexual rights, divorce, and witches. We now think differently on many issues.

We know these new things, and we can read the Bible and interpret its words accordingly and enjoy its ancient ambience.

The Bible tells us clearly that human selfishness (sin) is still the major concern to humanity and poses a grave risk to life as we know it on earth.

As I see it, believing in God as a higher authority, and the Bible as an inspirational guide for living, provides an effective way to discover real meaning and purpose in life. It defeats many of the 'demons' of modern living, mainly through a philosophy of service to others.

Regardless of how each of us understands God, 'God' can be seen in Jesus and what he taught. Reference to the above *Notes* provides substantial evidence that much of the teaching of Jesus was universal in character, applicable beyond limits of individual cultures and religions, and timeless. Through his teaching, we develop greater satisfaction in life and spiritual strengths. This message is repeated many times in the Gospels and by Paul and Peter in the *Letters*.

*

CONCLUSIONS

To end these Notes, it is useful to endorse the conclusions of a respected theologian.

I refer to Christine Pedotti, who was editor in chief of the magazine *Christian Witness* and is the author of many works on the Catholic Faith. Christine is the author of *Jesus: cet homme inconnu* (Jesus: the unknown man), published by XO Editions, Paris, in 2013.

Christine identifies the importance of Jesus' parable about Final Judgement, found in the New Testament (Matthew 22, 24 and 25), where Jesus speaks of the 'sheep':

"I was thirsty, and you gave me drink, hungry and you gave me food, I was a stranger and you welcomed me, without clothes and you clothed me, sick and you looked after me, in prison and you visited me."

Christine endorses my views – that Jesus' teaching is often universal in character and Jesus was not bothered whether a person called themselves a Jew or non-Jew and, by implication, Christian or non-Christian, or something else.

Christine Pedotti concludes that there is <u>nothing in Jesus' criteria that has anything to do with the exercise of religion in the ordinary sense of the word. What matters is what you do in life.</u>

The Letter of John, 4, v 20-21, sums it up:

"If someone says 'I love God' but detests his brother [neighbour] he is a liar . . . He who loves God must love his/ her neighbour."

As Pedotti rightly says: This ruins much contemporary religious activity.

I go to church to remind myself what I should believe, and to give myself a spiritual boost for the coming week.

Celebrating the birth story of Jesus at Christmas and proclaiming that 'Jesus is Risen!' on Easter Sunday reminds me that we all come to our beliefs in unique ways and interpret things differently.

It is how we put our faith into practice for the next seven days that matters. To my mind, the 'next world' is another story.

HARRY HOULDSWORTH, May 2022

*

SOURCES

The principal source used for these *Notes* is the Holy Bible.

I generally use the *Holy Bible*, New International Version, first published in 1979, with frequent cross references to the *Good News Bible*, first published in Britain in 1976.

For the *Notes* on the Synoptic Gospels of *Matthew, Mark,* and *Luke*, I have been guided by *Gospel Parallels – A Comparison of the Synoptic Gospels*, by Thomas Nelson Publishers, 1992 edition.

Gospel Parallels permits an instant comparison of the individual treatment of the stories in the three early Gospels in the *New Testament*.

Gospel Parallels is a useful reference source for those wishing to read the original Bible passages referred to in these *Notes*. Alternatively, reference can be made to the Gospels of *Matthew, Mark, Luke,* and *John*, in any popular edition of the *New Testament*.

For further reading of any of the topics in these *Notes*, refer to the *New Bible Commentary, 21st Century Edition*.

I use the 1994 edition published by Inter-varsity Press, Leicester, England, but any other edition provides detailed comments on orthodox interpretations of passages in the *Bible*.

Linked to these *Gospel Notes* is *Jesus' Story – For a Thoughtful Generation*, by Harry Houldsworth, privately-published in 2020, and now available from the author. Email houldken@gmail.com for further information.

Gospel Notes is mainly a personal testimony, based on the Bible, but I do make incidental reference to the following books:

Michael Grant, *Jesus,* Weidenfield & Nicholson, 1977.

H A Guy, *The Acts of the Apostles,* Macmillam & Co., 1953

Christine Pedotti, *Jesus: cet homme Inconnu,* XO Editions, Paris, 2013.

*

CPSIA information can be obtained
at www.ICGtesting.com
Printed in the USA
LVHW031913160922
728572LV00003B/198

9 781803 811451